How to Pass

English for Business

Level 2

4TH EDITION

How to Pass English for Business Level 2

4th Edition 2011 Reprint 2015, 2018 und 2019

ISBN 978-3-922514-29-9

Published by: **Logophon-Verlag GmbH**
Hauptstr. 23, 63811 Stockstadt
Tel: 0 60 27 / 4188-820
Fax: 0 60 27 / 4188-40
E-Mail: verlag@logophon.de
Website: www.logophon.de

OTHER BUSINESS ENGLISH TITLES PUBLISHED BY LOGOPHON VERLAG GMBH:

How to Pass English for Business Preliminary Level	ISBN 978-3-922514-27-5
How to Pass English for Business Level 1	ISBN 978-3-922514-28-2
How to Pass English for Business Level 2	ISBN 978-3-922514-29-9
How to Pass English for Business Level 3	ISBN 978-3-922514-32-9

How to Pass Spoken English for Industry and Commerce PRELIMINARY Level

Student's Book	ISBN 3-922514-33-2
Teacher's Book	ISBN 3-922514-37-5
Picture Book	ISBN 3-922514-39-1

How to Pass Spoken English for Industry and Commerce THRESHOLD Level

Student's Book	ISBN 3-922514-34-0
Teacher's Book	ISBN 3-922514-40-5
Picture Book	ISBN 3-922514-42-1

How to Pass Spoken English for Industry and Commerce INTERMEDIATE Level

Student's Book	ISBN 3-922514-35-9
Student's CD	ISBN 3-922514-44-8
Teacher's Book	ISBN 3-922514-43-x

How to Pass Spoken English for Industry and Commerce ADVANCED Level

Student's Book	ISBN 3-922514-36-7
Student's CD	ISBN 3-922514-46-4
Teacher's Book	ISBN 3-922514-45-6

Business English Tests	ISBN 3-922514-91-x
More Business English Tests	ISBN 3-922514-92-8
Advanced Business English Tests	ISBN 3-922514-93-6

CONTENTS

INTRODUCTION

This book is the official examination preparation book for the LCCI English for Business Level 2 examination. It uses practice examination questions to prepare candidates for the English for Business Level 2 written examination. Guidance in how to approach the questions is provided, followed by controlled practice, revision tests and further practice. Two complete examination papers are included; one at the beginning to show students what the exam looks like as a whole and one at the end to provide a mock examination which can be carried out under exam conditions. Further past papers are available from www.lccieb-germany.com or www.lcci.org.uk

This book can be used either as a class book or for self-study. On the next pages you will find information about the compulsory written examination and the optional speaking and listening tests.

The **MAIN SECTION** of the book consists of 7 sections which cover the examination tasks, as follows:

- **Memos**
- **Leaflets**
- **Notices**
- **Reports**
- **Articles**
- **Lists**
- **Letters**

Each section has an introduction, which explains the six-stage approach to answering the questions. The six stages are:

1. Identify the task
2. Layout
3. Identify relevant information
4. Group/order relevant information
5. Write the answer
6. Check your work

This is followed by an example in which the six stages have already been completed. A second example is provided for the student to complete the six stages and write the answer. Following the student's example are six further questions providing more practice material.

Answers to the questions in sections 1-7 can be found at the back of the book in the section entitled '**ANSWERS: SECTIONS 1-7.**'

A **REVISION TEST** is provided which uses material from the given examples in each section and requires the student to answer all 7 types of questions; memo, leaflet, notice, report, article, list, letter. The **REVISION TEST ANSWERS** are contained in the completed example at the front of each section.

Following the revision test is a section entitled '**FURTHER PRACTICE**.' This provides 20 further questions requiring students to write memos, leaflets, notices, reports, articles, lists and letters.

Answers to the further practice questions can be found at the back of the book in the section entitled '**ANSWERS: FURTHER PRACTICE.**'

A '**GLOSSARY'** section at the back of the book lists the main words used in the book.

Finally, '**SAMPLE EXAMINATION PAPER 2'** provides a complete examination which can be held under exam conditions.

Answers to both examination papers can be found at the back of the book.

THE COMPULSORY WRITTEN EXAMINATION

The English for Business Level 2 written examination lasts for 2 hours and 30 minutes It consists of 3 questions. Question 1 carries 30 marks, Question 2 carries 40 marks and Question 3 carries 30 marks. The total number of marks available is 100. Candidates must achieve 50 marks overall to pass. Credit is awarded to candidates gaining over 60% and Distinction is awarded to candidates gaining over 75%.

Question 1 is an extended writing task requiring candidates to produce ONE of the following; a memorandum, an article, a report, a leaflet, a notice, etc, on a choice of role-related topics drawn from business and economic life. Candidates have to answer 1 question from a choice of 3. In Question 1 candidates should display the virtues of good non-literary writing – order, clarity, balance, relevance, economy, accuracy and logic. The tasks will require candidates to adopt office roles and write to identified addressees within a defined situation.

Question 2 is a letter writing task, where the stimulus is in the form of an incoming business letter. In Question 2 examiners will accept a variety of current business letter layouts, provided they are followed consistently. Layouts other than those outlined in this book are permissible as long as they help the clarity of the communication and are among the styles commonly used in business.

Question 3 is a reformulation task requiring candidates to expand, reduce or selectively rewrite a passage of English for some defined purpose within a given role. Candidates will be offered tasks that will draw on their ability to make notes, or reassemble elements of a text for a specific purpose, which will be stated. Questions 1 and 3 often require types of outcome which are similar to each other. Although the task in question 3 is usually a list, it can also be a memorandum, an article, a report, a leaflet, or a notice. Whereas the emphasis in Question 1 is on skills such as clarity, economy etc, the emphasis in Question 3 is on the skills of rewriting and reorganisation.

In general marks are awarded for: content, accuracy in spelling, layout, punctuation and grammar. Additionally marks are awarded for the satisfactory completion of the communicative task, which will depend on the appropriateness of the candidate's choice of tone, style, length and format.
A typical weighting of marks for a complete written paper would be:

- clarity and appropriacy of layout 20%
- style, tone, suitability to the task 30%
- content and communication of message 20%
- accuracy of grammar, spelling etc 30%

Where possible candidates should avoid copying whole phrases or sentences from the examination paper.An Infopack (including exam syllabus) and Past Paper Packs are available from www.lccieb-germany.com.

OPTIONAL SPEAKING TEST

An optional Speaking Test is available for English for Business Level 2. Candidates will be assessed by a 13 minute examination including 5 minutes preparation time. Candidates will be assessed on four criteria – fluency, lexis, grammar and pronunciation. The examination consists of 2 parts as follows:

Part 1 consists of a warm up conversation during which the candidate will be asked about general topics, eg. study, work ambitions for the future.

Part 2 requires the candidate to participate in a discussion of the topic selected by the examiner.

More information can be found on the next pages and a guidance document for examiners and tutorial CD is available from www.lccieb-germany.com or www.lcci.org.uk

OPTIONAL LISTENING TEST

An optional Listening Test is available for English for Business Level 2. Candidates will be assessed by a 20 minute examination consisting of 30 multiple choice questions.
There are two types of tasks:

Task 1 (10 questions). Candidates listen to a recorded question, which has three recorded responses (A, B, C) and candidates choose the appropriate response.

Task 2 (20 questions). Candidates listen to short conversations or announcements. They then read a question about the conversation or announcement, which has four possible responses (A, B, C, D), and choose the appropriate response.

More information can be found on the next pages and a guidance document for examiners and tutorial CD is available from www.lccieb-germany.com or www.lcci.org.uk

THE OPTIONAL SPEAKING TEST

The Speaking Test is optional. At Level 2 the Speaking Test lasts 13 minutes. There are 3 parts as follows;

- **Preparation 5 minutes**
  You will be given a sheet which states the TOPIC and provides some questions or statements about the topic. You have 5 minutes to read the questions or statements and think about what you are going to say.

- **Warm up 2 minutes**
  During the warm-up the examiner will ask you about general information, eg (background, study, work, ambitions for the future)

- **Examination 6 minutes**
  The examiner will ask you some of the questions about the topic. The themes will be of general interest, eg;
  - EARNING A LIVING (eg wages, living standards, types of work, health & safety, etc)
  - PRODUCTION AND SALE OF GOODS (distribution, retail/wholesale, consumer rights, etc)
  - TRADE (eg import/export, international trade, globalisation, etc)
  - MONEY (eg methods of payment, inflation, banking services, savings, pensions, etc)
  - TRANSPORT (eg types of transport, uses, problems)
  - COMMUNICATIONS (eg media, internet, TV, telephones, newspapers, etc)
  - EDUCATION AND TRAINING (eg your education, education systems, training, etc)
  - TRAVEL AND TOURISM (eg methods of transport, role of travel in modern life, tourism, etc)

You will be tested for;
- Fluency
- Vocabulary
- Grammar
- Pronunciation

The grades awarded are;
- Pass with Distinction (=Excellent)
- Pass with Credit (=Very good)
- Pass
- Fail

Typical Warm-up Questions

What's your first name? How do you spell it? What is your family name? Do you have a middle name?
How old are you? When is your birthday? What is your date of birth?
Where were you born? Where are you from? Where did you go to school?
Where did you learn English? Why are you learning English? How often do you speak English?
What other languages can you speak? Where did you learn these?
What were your favourite subjects at school? What did you do after school?
Are you at college? What are you learning? How long is the course? What will you do after college?
Do you work? What do you do?
Where do you work? When did you start work there? Why did you choose this job?
What training do you have for this job? Do you get regular training?
Where did you work before that? How long will you stay in this job? With this company?
What possibilities are there in your job for the future? What are your career ambitions?
Where do you live? Is it a nice place? Why did you choose to live there?
What do you do in your spare time?
Do you have any family? What do they do? Where do they live?
Do you have any hobbies? What are they? What do you enjoy about your hobbies?
Have you ever been to an English-Speaking country? Where? How long ago was it? What did you do there?
Where would you like to go for your next holiday? Why?
Where did you go on your last holiday? Why did you choose this place?
What are your ambitions in your private life?

SAMPLE TOPIC 1 : HEALTH & SAFETY AT WORK

(Syllabus Topic: Earning a Living)

Please note that pictures are NOT part of the speaking test at Level 2 and are only provided in this preparation book as a stimulus for the topic and to encourage students to speak.

- Describe what you can see in the picture.
- What in your opinion does the phrase "a safe working environment" mean.
- Comment on how this can be applied to:
  - Office Furniture
  - Heating, lighting, ventilation
  - Machinery and equipment
  - Fire risks
  - Accident risks
- Now comment on the above in relation to the picture.
- Explain where you work and what you do. Suggest any improvements which would make a safer working environment at your place of work. What procedures are in place in the event of an accident at work? Have you ever had an accident at work? Why is it important to prevent accidents at work for the employer? For the employee?

SAMPLE TOPIC 2 : INTERNATIONAL AID & TRADE

(Syllabus Topic: Trade)

Give an example of a country which has food shortages, a low standard of living and low levels of welfare support. What do you know about the situation? What are the reasons for the situation? How can the situation be improved?
In what ways could richer countries help?
What are the advantages and disadvantages of the following methods of help;

- Donating money to a charity
- Providing grants for training, eg agricultural colleges
- Donating food supplies, equipment, medical supplies, etc
- Providing facilities for training, eg funding schools and colleges

What do you understand by the phrase "Trade not Aid." Do you agree that it is better to trade with such countries than to give money? Why? Why not?

SAMPLE TOPIC 3 : METHODS OF COMMUNICATION

(Syllabus Topic: Communications)

- What is happening in the picture? What methods of communication are being used?
- You work in an office and have been asked to contact all sales staff to arrange a meeting next week. How many different ways of contacting them are there? What are the advantages and disadvantages of each? What factors would affect your decision?
- Look at the methods of communication below, explain them and give examples of situations in which a company would use them:

➤ Telephone (Landline, Mobile, Internet)	➤ Normal post
➤ Teleconference / Videoconference	➤ Express courier
➤ Email	➤ Fax
➤ SMS	➤ Registered post

SAMPLE TOPIC 4 : PAYMENT OF GOODS

(Syllabus Topic: Money)

How many different ways are there to pay for goods? As an individual? As a company?

What is the best way as an individual if you are buying something from:

- a shop in your home town?
- a shop while you are on holiday in a foreign country?
- a mail order catalogue?
- the internet?

What is the best way for a company to pay for goods from:

- A regular supplier in the same country? In a foreign country?
- A new supplier in the same country ? in a foreign country?

What risks are involved and how can the company minimise the risks?

SAMPLE TOPIC 5 : TELEVISION AND ITS ROLE TODAY
(Syllabus Topic: Communications)

Do you have a television? How much time do you spend watching it a day? a week?
What percentage of people in your country have a television?
How can television be used:

- to inform
- to educate
- to entertain
- to advertise (adverts, product placement, endorsements)

How can television influence people positively?
How can television influence people negatively?
Is the importance of television increasing or decreasing? Why do you think this is?

SAMPLE TOPIC 6 : THE ORIGIN OF GOODS
(Syllabus Topic: Production and Sale of Goods)

- What are you wearing? What are you carrying? Choose one item and explain the following; What is it? What is it made from? What do you know about its origins? What raw materials are used? Where was it made? How was it made? What processes are involved in the production of it? How many countries were involved in the making of the product? What transport is involved between the raw materials and the destination of the product?

- Think about this on a general level. Is the distance between the origin and the destination of goods getting bigger or smaller? Are certain industries more affected than others, eg food production, clothing manufacturing, automobile industry, technological products, pharmaceutical industries. Why (not)? What is your opinion on this?

- How do you think it will develop in the next 20 years?

LISTENING TEST

The Listening Test is optional. At Level 2 it will test whether a candidate can:

- understand the main points of clear standard speech regularly encountered in work and everyday life, including short narratives, though will sometimes need to ask for repetition or clarification.
- understand straightforward, factual information about common, everyday or job-related topics, identifying both general topic and specific detail, provided the speech is clearly articulated.
- understand simple technical information, such as operating instructions, and can follow detailed directions.
- follow in outline straightforward short talks on familiar topics.
- follow a straightforward and clearly structured lecture or talk within his / her field.
- understand the main points of radio news bulletins.
- understand the information content of the majority of broadcast audio material on topics of personal interest delivered in a relatively slow and clear standard speech.

The grades awarded are;

- Pass with Distinction (=Excellent)
- Pass with Credit (=Very good)
- Pass
- Fail

The Level 2 Listening Test lasts 20 minutes. There are 30 questions in total. All 30 questions are multiple-choice.

You will be given a booklet containing the questions and an answer sheet with space to mark your answers, like this.

1	A	B	C	D		6	A	B	C	D
2	A	B	C	D		7	A	B	C	D
3	A	B	C	D		8	A	B	C	D
4	A	B	C	D		9	A	B	C	D
5	A	B	C	D		10	A	B	C	D

You should use a pencil to mark your answers like this:

1	●	B	C	D		6	A	B	●	D
2	A	●	C	D		7	A	●	C	D
3	●	B	C	D		8	A	B	●	D
4	A	B	C	●		9	●	B	C	D
5	A	B	C	●		10	A	B	C	●

The Level 2 Listening Test consists of 2 parts as follows;

Part 1 Question and correct response (10 questions)

Part 2 a) Conversation and correct responses (15 questions)
b) Monologue and correct response (5 questions)

On the next pages you will find examples of the types of questions in each part of the test.

SAMPLE QUESTIONS

Part 1

In Part 1 you will hear a question and then hear three possible responses (A, B or C). You should choose the correct response.

Question 1

A	Man: Woman:	So what do you do? What's your job? I've got a meeting with the Sales Director in 5 minutes.
B	Man: Woman:	So what do you do? What's your job? I'm a sales representative for an electronics company.
C	Man: Woman:	So what do you do? What's your job? I have to travel a lot more than I used to.

The correct answer is B.

Question 2

A	Man: Woman:	What time did she say she'd arrive? We should get there by about three.
B	Man: Woman:	What time did she say she'd arrive? You can drive but it's much quicker to fly.
C	Man: Woman:	What time did she say she'd arrive? I think she should be here at about 3 o'clock.

The correct answer is C.

PART 2

In Part 2a of the test there is a question in your booklet with four possible answers. You read the question and then listen for the answer. You will hear a short conversation or announcement.

Question: How much does one shirt cost?

A. £9.00
B. £10.50
C. £21.00
D. £30.00

Recorded conversation:

Woman:	Excuse me, can you tell me how much this shirt costs?
Man:	It's £10.50.
Woman:	OK, I'll take a blue one and a red one.
Man:	Fine, that's £21 please.
Woman:	Here's £30.
Man:	Thank you. And here's £9 change.

The correct answer is B

In Part 2b of the test there is a question in your booklet with four possible answers. You then listen to the conversation for the correct answer.

Question: What kind of problem is being discussed?
A. A personnel problem.
B. A legal problem.
C. A supply problem.
D. An electrical problem.

Recorded conversation:

Man:	There's a problem with the light in the corridor – sometimes it works and sometimes it doesn't.
Woman:	I know. It's probably something to do with the switch. I'll ask the caretaker to see if he can fix it.
Man:	Good – but in the meantime maybe we should put a notice on the door warning employees about it – we don't want somebody breaking their leg and then taking us to court.

The correct answer is D

Question: What are MX Technologies going to do?
A. Lower the price of their microchips.
B. Open a new factory in Poland.
C. Take on 500 new employees.
D. Move their employees to a new site.

Recorded conversation:

And now to business news. The microchip company MX Technologies have today announced that they are closing their factory in Scotland and moving their main production site to Poland due to lower labour costs in eastern Europe. It is feared that over 500 employees could lose their jobs as a result of the move.

The correct answer is B

Question: What is the woman going to check?
A. The address of Friedel Lights.
B. The cost of sending the order by courier.
C. How they normally send orders to this client.
D. Whether to send the order by post or by courier.

Woman	*Excuse me Jim. You know the order for Friedel Lights?*
Man	*Yes, the one that came in by fax?*
Woman	*Yes, that's right, do you know if they want the order sending by courier or by post?*
Man	*Well, I spoke to Mrs. Friedel this morning and she didn't mention it. It is safer to send it by courier though.*
Woman	*OK- I'd better check, as that'll work out quite a lot more expensive.*
Man	*Yes, that would be a good idea.*

The correct answer is B

Sample Examination Paper 1

ENGLISH FOR BUSINESS

Level 2

Subject Code: 2041

Time allowed: **2 hours 30 minutes**

INSTRUCTIONS FOR CANDIDATES

- Answer **all 3** questions. You should only answer **one** option in **question 1**.
- All answers should be correctly numbered, but do not need to be in numerical order.
- There is credit for correct spelling, punctuation and grammar.
- You need to communicate appropriately and well.
- Check your work carefully.
- You may use an English or bilingual dictionary.

QUESTION 1

Write on ONE of the following options:

Option (a)

Setting

Mrs Grace Harris, Managing Director of Sure Solutions in Birmingham, England talks with you about the new offices being set up in Casablanca, Morocco. Part of the conversation is:

Mrs Harris:	You know that we are opening a new office in Morocco – well, several of our senior staff will have to visit Casablanca to interview new staff, check the building work, order stock ... you know the sort of thing!
You:	We have a committee that is working out details of the project.
Mrs Harris:	Of course ... you are chairperson of the committee. I had forgotten.
You:	Yes. We have made a list of some facts and arrangements to help our colleagues who visit Casablanca – they are very simple pieces of information.
Mrs Harris:	I am in a hurry at the moment, but I would like to see what information you already have.
You:	I have some notes ...
Mrs Harris:	Oh, sorry. I hate notes. I can never understand them. **Write a memo** to me.

Here are the notes that you have made:

Visa – not needed for British citizens BUT passport – valid 6 months (at least) after arrival in Morocco. Must have RETURN ticket!

Expect French to be spoken (few Moroccans speak English) – Yves Roland is our resident representative in Casablanca – fluent English and French – I have details for contact.

Recommend Hotel Le Royal Mansour (Casablanca) - I have details for contact.

Casablanca – direct flight from Birmingham – journey about 5 hours.
(Airport – 40 minutes in taxi to hotel.)

Task

Write the memo. **(40 marks)**

Option (b)

Setting

You work at Greenfield Public Library where you have responsibility for the Children's Library. During the past month, all older children using the Children's Library, and adults accompanying younger children, have been asked to write down any comments they wish to make and to suggest improvements on what is offered to them. You have to **write a report** on the findings for the next meeting of the Library Committee.

Here are your notes:

300 users answered (212 older children/88 adults)

Some (adults and children) complained about times of opening.

> *At present Children's Library opens 1 hour after Main Library – closes 1 hour before Main Library – users want us to open (and close) at the same times.*

Lack of space to study – older children want to do homework - one table only + six chairs!

Can we open a separate study-room? Present Children's Library is far too small.

Lack of computer facilities – one computer = not enough.

REQUESTS for:
- *more computers*
- *easier use of photocopier (at present – users have to ask a member of staff for permission)*

MOST ADULTS ARE SATISFIED WITH FACILITIES FOR YOUNGER CHILDREN.
(In particular they like the Saturday morning story-telling.)

Older children complain of noise from younger children AND FROM ADULTS!

Task

Write the report. **(40 marks)**

Option (c)

Setting

You work in a large department store in your own town or city. A recent issue of the staff magazine announces that a new brochure about the store is being designed. It will be sent to anyone who applies for a job at the store. Part of the announcement reads, "We need current employees to write articles that we can use in the brochure. If you are interested, write an article, 4 or 5 paragraphs long, describing what it is like to work in our store."

You decide that you want to **write an article** for the magazine.

Here are some notes that you make of possible ideas to include:

Tiring BUT worthwhile *different people – customers and colleagues*

range of goods *people who can't decide what to buy* *being patient*

keeping self and goods looking tidy *debit and credit cards*

(I may want to add other ideas and/or miss some out.)

Task

Write the article. **(40 marks)**

QUESTION 2

You work at Joynton Electrical and Electronic Supplies. Miss Elaine Walsh, Manager, gives you the following letter and asks you to **write a letter** in reply. She says, “The Erskineville Branch was where we had the huge fire. Check if we know anything about Mrs Kemmis’s radio ... Woolloomalloo Branch could have been more helpful ... Everything that we could salvage was sent there. Apologise to Mrs Kemmis ... If her radio was badly damaged, offer to replace it.”

19 Lawson Square
Redfern
New South Wales 2012

April 3 ....

Joynton Electrical and Electronic Supplies
43 Kent Street
Sydney
New South Wales 2000

Dear Sir or Madam

Radio – left for repair at Joynton EES (Erskineville Branch)

Three months ago, I left a radio to be repaired at your Erskineville Branch. About a week later I received a phone-call saying that it was ready for collection. Unfortunately, that day I became ill and had to spend 2 weeks in hospital.

When I recovered, I tried to collect the radio. The Erskineville Branch was closed and on the door was a handwritten notice stating that all business had been transferred to the Woolloomalloo Branch. I wrote to that Branch and eventually after 3 further letters enquiring about my property, I received a telephoned reply saying that I should write to the Sydney Head Office.

I think that I should have been contacted personally by Joynton EES and that I should not have to travel all over the Sydney area of Australia trying to get my belongings back.

I would appreciate an early reply.

Yours faithfully

Marcelle Kemmis

Marcelle Kemmis (Mrs)

You telephone Woolloomalloo Branch.

The Manager of the Branch says, “What? We only got one letter and a very rude phone-call. I told her to contact you because she became angry when I said that her radio must have been badly damaged in the fire. She did not believe me when I told her that we could not contact her because the fire had destroyed our computer records and our paper files. She would not listen to me and kept shouting, ‘Where is my radio?’”

Mrs Kemmis needs to give you details of her radio: make, model etc so that you can replace it. You think, “I must be tactful. She is clearly very upset. Perhaps, I can offer to deliver it free of charge.”

Task

Write the letter. **(30 marks)**

QUESTION 3

Remember that in Question 3 you should use your own words whenever possible and appropriate.

Setting

You are the Development and Training Manager of a large, international furnishing store. The directors have asked you to submit a plan to aim sales more specifically towards certain groups of customer. You find an article in a magazine and part of it seems to have ideas that will be suitable for the plan. **Write a list** of the main points from this extract of the article:

SENIOR CUSTOMERS

We often read that the average age of the population in many countries is rising very quickly. In some countries, the number of people over the age of 65 is increasing 3 times faster than any other age group. They now represent the fastest growing group of consumers. The older generation is made up generally of people who are loyal customers and who appreciate it when companies obviously set out to be attractive to them.

What is your business doing to attract these consumers?

Older consumers look for service after sales. Businesses need to contact their "senior customers" to see how the product or service has suited them. Genuine guarantees of the product, the workmanship and the satisfaction of the consumer are also essential. More than any other age group, the over 65s will accept that a product and/or service may go wrong, but they expect the problem to be put right immediately and without argument.

You must train your sales team to deal with older consumers. Provide a quiet place in which to discuss a sale. If possible, supply written information about the product /service. Above all tell your staff to forget their usual sales' techniques. The older consumer likes time in which to think, and honest information NOT 'sales-talk'.

If you want to encourage this valued group of potential buyers to want what you are offering, don't forget to place your advertisements sensibly in media that are likely to be used by the more mature person, and use models who themselves belong to the age group.

Task

Write the list. **(30 marks)**

Answers to Sample Examination Paper 1 can be found on pages 169-173.

SECTIONS
1 – 7

SECTION 1: MEMOS

STAGE 1: IDENTIFY THE TASK

Read the question and work out exactly what you are required to do. The instruction at the bottom of the question normally reads "Write the memo." Note any additional instructions, eg "Write the memo tactfully."

STAGE 2: LAYOUT

A memo requires the following information:

- Who is the memo to?
- Who is the memo from?
- What is the memo about?
- What is the date?

This information should be positioned at the start of the memo. Two examples of layout are below. A job position may be added after the name of the sender (and/or recipient), eg To: James Douglas, Sales Director From: Jan Robins, Sales Manager. The initials of the writer may also be added at the bottom of the memo, eg J.R. Using paragraphs for different points is recommended.

MEMO

To: James Douglas, Sales Director
From: Jan Robins, Sales Manager
Subject: Meeting on 10 September
Date: Today's date

....
....
....

....
....
J.R.

MEMO

To James Douglas
From Jan Robins
Date Today's date

Meeting on 10 September

....
....
......

....
....

STAGE 3: IDENTIFY RELEVANT INFORMATION

A memo is usually fairly short. It should include enough so that the correct information is communicated, but should not include anything extra to this.

STAGE 4: GROUP/ORDER RELEVANT INFORMATION

The information and notes given are often in a suitable order. If the information is not in a suitable order, it is useful to group points relating to the same subject together.

STAGE 5: WRITE THE MEMO

The language used in memos is shorter and more direct than in letters. It is important to stay to the point, but be polite. Watch out for extra instructions, such as "Be tactful." Make sure that the person who receives the memo will be able to understand the message.

STAGE 6: CHECK YOUR WORK

CHECKLIST: MEMOS

1 Have you completed the task? (Will the person who receives the memo understand the message?)
2 Is the layout correct?
3 Are the details correct (To: From: Date:)?
4 Does the subject line tell you briefly what the memo is about?
5 Have you included all the relevant information?
6 Have you ordered the information in the best way?
7 Is the language appropriate for a memo?
8 Have you checked spelling, grammar and punctuation?

COMPLETED EXAMPLE

Setting: You work at RJS Cutting Machines, a company which manufactures and services fabric cutting machines.

You have just received a telephone call from Mr Lawdon, an important customer, who is very unhappy. Last week Mr Lawdon bought two machines from your company. Both the machines have broken down and you have agreed to go to his factory first thing in the morning to try and repair the machines. Write a memo to your assistant, Steve Hill, explaining why you will be out of the office tomorrow and asking him to carry out the duties listed below. Tell him you should be back in the office by mid-afternoon.

TO DO LIST

- *Phone Andrew (Engineering Dept.) - explain situation, say I might call for help.*
- *Phone Susan (Planning Dept) - ask for availability on new FXL 9000 cutting machine.*
- *Meeting at 10 am - Karen Locke (Ingar Co.) - new customer*
  - show round factory, demonstrate FXL 9000.
- *FXL 7500 model - Find out if situation with faulty components has been resolved.*
  If yes, find out delivery time. Valerie will know (Ext. 459).

Write the memo.

STAGE 1: IDENTIFY THE TASK
Write the memo.

STAGE 2: LAYOUT

To:	Steve Hill
From:	Your name
Subject:	Things to do tomorrow in my absence
Date:	Today's date

STAGE 3: IDENTIFY RELEVANT INFORMATION

- say why you're not in office tomorrow and reason
- jobs you had planned and now require Steve to do
- telephone Andrew (Engineering) explain situation/might call
- telephone Susan (Planning) availability FXL 9000
- 10 am meeting Karen Locke (Ingar Co.) new customer / show around / demonstrate FXL 9000
- telephone Valerie (Ext. 459) situation faulty components FXL 7500
- also delivery time FXL 7500
- when you should be back

STAGE 4: GROUP/ORDER RELEVANT INFORMATION

1 Your absence from office tomorrow and the reason.
2 The jobs you had planned and now require Steve to do.
3 Telephone Andrew (Engineering). Explain where you are and why you might call.
4 Telephone Susan (Planning). Ask about the availability of new FXL 9000.
5 10 am meeting with Karen Locke (Ingar Co.). She is a new customer, show her around and demonstrate the FXL 9000.
6 Telephone Valerie (Ext. 459). Ask if situation with faulty components FXL 7500 has been resolved. Also for delivery time of FXL 7500?
7 Should be back in the office by mid-afternoon.

STAGE 5: WRITE THE MEMO

MEMO

To: Steve Hill
From: Your name
Subject: Things to do tomorrow in my absence
Date: Today's date

Mr Lawdon has just been on the telephone.

Both the machines he bought last week have broken down and I have agreed to visit him tomorrow morning to try and repair them.

In my absence I would like you to take care of a number of things for me.

1 Telephone Andrew in Engineering.

Explain where I have gone and why. Tell him I might need to call for his help.

2 Telephone Susan in Planning.

Ask her about the availability of the new FXL 9000 cutting machine.

3 Take my meeting at 10 am.

I have a meeting at 10 am with Karen Locke from Ingar Co, who are new customers. Make my apologies, show her around the factory and demonstrate the new FXL 9000 cutting machine.

4 Telephone Valerie on Ext. 459.

Ask if the situation with the faulty components on the FXL 7500 has been resolved. Also ask her what the delivery time is for the FXL 7500.

I should be back in the office by mid-afternoon.

STAGE 6: CHECK YOUR WORK

CHECKLIST: MEMOS

1	Have you completed the task?	✓
2	Is the layout correct?	✓
3	Are the details correct (To: From: Date:)?	✓
4	Does the subject line tell you briefly what the memo is about?	✓
5	Have you included all the relevant information?	✓
6	Have you ordered the information in the best way?	✓
7	Is the language appropriate for a memo?	✓
8	Have you checked spelling, grammar and punctuation?	✓

YOUR EXAMPLE

Situation: You work in the Administration Department of a gold mine belonging to AG Corporation, an international mining company. Michael Rosselini is the Manager.

You have just returned from lunch to find the following note from Mr Rosselini on your desk.

Just heard that Aaron Jackson, Chief Executive Officer, is visiting next Tuesday. Write a memo from me to all staff re situation. Visit from 11 to 3. He's interested in the new gold we struck 2 days ago. He'll probably just be in meetings with management, but might want to go into mine / talk to staff. First time he's visited so important that we give a good impression.

Write the memo.

STAGE 1: IDENTIFY THE TASK

....

STAGE 2: LAYOUT

To: ....

From: ....

Subject: ....

Date: ....

STAGE 3: IDENTIFY RELEVANT INFORMATION

....

....

....

....

....

....

....

....

....

....

STAGE 4: GROUP/ORDER RELEVANT INFORMATION

....

....

....

....

....

....

....

....

....

....

STAGE 5: WRITE THE MEMO

STAGE 6: CHECK YOUR WORK

CHECKLIST: MEMOS

1	Have you completed the task?	
2	Is the layout correct?	
3	Are the details correct (To: From: Date:)?	
4	Does the subject line tell you briefly what the memo is about?	
5	Have you included all the relevant information?	
6	Have you ordered the information in the best way?	
7	Is the language appropriate for a memo?	
8	Have you checked spelling, grammar and punctuation?	

PRACTICE 1

Setting: You work in the office of Maple Garages, the main Ford car dealer in Norwich.

The contractors who are redecorating your customer reception area have told you that they will need an extra day to finish the job. They had planned to be finished on Sunday night but will not be finished now until Monday evening. As a result the customer reception area will be closed on Monday. Write a memo to all staff informing them of the situation. Explain that customer access will have to be through the workshop and make the following points.

- Don't obstruct passageways.
- Be friendly and helpful to customers.
- Avoid oil spills
- Be careful when backing cars out of garage
- Keep the music turned down a bit.

Write the memo.

PRACTICE 2

Situation: You work in the Head Office of Anglo Energy plc.

Mrs Hasten, Personnel Manager, says, "Christmas is rapidly approaching and we need to know who is going to be on holiday and when. Can you write a memo to all staff for me based on these notes I've made?" Here are Mrs Hasten's notes.

Already December - time to plan Christmas holidays. All staff who want holidays - contact Simon in Admin Dept (Room 245 tel. Ext. 450) asap. Need to know dates requested. All holiday leave must be taken by Dec 31 - can't be paid out. Add that Dec 25 and 26 are public holidays and not deducted from annual leave.

Write the memo.

PRACTICE 3

Setting: You are PA to Mr Robert Principal, Chairman of Atlantic Pharmaceuticals Co.

The extended credit facility, which the company had with its bank, was terminated yesterday. This means that the company can't operate any longer. This morning the receivers were called in to take over the company. The Chairman has asked you to write a memo in his name to all staff informing them of what has happened. He asks you to include the following points.

Situation has arisen because of loss of major customers abroad due to strong pound / loss of many UK customers now buying their goods abroad (taking advantage of strong pound) rather than from us. Hope no jobs will be lost. Hope to find a buyer to take over whole company. In the meantime "business as usual." As soon as more details are known will inform staff.

Write the memo.

PRACTICE 4

Situation: You are Customer Services Manager at the Head Office of Lawson Shoes, a High Street shoe retailer.

You are getting a lot of complaints from customers who have tried to exchange shoes or get a refund and who have been turned away. Write a memo to all retail staff informing them of the company's policy using the notes below.

Tell customers - keep receipt.
Inform them - come back within 10 days if not satisfied.
Procedure:
- ask to see receipt - check date / check shoes (new? worn? still in box?)
- is receipt for shoes? If OK - offer refund / exchange (shoes can be different type/ price/ etc).
- **Note**: no refunds for sales goods!
Exchange of sales goods = only for other sales goods of same price.

Write the memo.

PRACTICE 5

Situation: Mr. Gulam Miah, a director of the firm for which you work, says, "I am concerned that some of our heads of department and team leaders have forgotten how to hold meetings efficiently. Do you realise that many of the meetings here go on for longer than 2 hours? It's ridiculous ... a good chairperson should ... well, I don't need to tell you! Your meetings are excellent. Will you write a memo to all heads of department and team leaders? Tell them how to improve their meetings ..."

Here are some notes that you make:

A good meeting =
agenda + precise/clear + everyone participates + STARTS ON TIME! - VERY strict on time (AND FINISHES ON - or before -TIME!)

AGENDA - Don't wander away from it - wanted BEFORE the meeting - circulate (BEFORE MEETING = most important.)

REASON = chance to think about what is to be discussed.

INVOLVE EVERYONE - "What do you think?" "Do we all agree?" etc

CHAIRPERSON keeps discussion relevant. "That's interesting, but can we look at it another time?"

Start on time! Waiting for people = encourage lateness.

Keep it short! Success = participation and decision NOT length of time

Write the memo.

PRACTICE 6

Situation:

You work at the Head Office of Peerless Commodities, Claremorris, County Mayo, Ireland. Here is a transcript of a telephone conversation that you had today with Mrs. Bridget Molloy, the Administrative Manager:

Mrs. Molloy	Hello. Will you write a memo to all the staff at Head Office, please? I should have written it earlier, but I have been delayed at our branch in Drogheda.
You	Of course I shall, Mrs. Molloy. What is the message?
Mrs. Molloy	Well, as you know, we have recently appointed a new Public Relations Officer, Miss Maureen Flavell ... No, I'm sorry ... It's not Flavell ...It's Flaherty. I'll spell her name: F...L...A...H...E...R...T...Y.
You	Yes, I met her after the interview.
Mrs. Molloy	She is coming next week to visit Peerless Commodities to look around our factory and offices. She wants to get some ideas of what may interest the newspapers, TV companies, magazines ... things that will be good publicity for us. She will visit on Tuesday. She'll arrive in the morning, at about 10 o'clock. Can you make certain that there is a car parking space reserved for her?
You	When does she begin her job?
Mrs. Molloy	Oh, it's not for another 6 weeks, but she wants to make plans before she officially starts. Will you show her around on Tuesday? Be her guide and introduce her to staff. She wants to talk with as many people as possible and to get ideas from them for possible publicity.

Write the memo and warn staff to expect the visit. It will be completely informal.

SECTION 2: LEAFLETS

STAGE 1: IDENTIFY THE TASK
Read the question and work out exactly what you are required to do. The instruction at the bottom of the question normally reads "Draft the leaflet" or "Write the leaflet."

STAGE 2: LAYOUT
There are no special rules for layout, however, a leaflet should be easy to read, eye-catching and contain contact details and a date. Layout of leaflets can be improved by:

- centralising text
- writing important information in capital letters
- keeping sentences short
- using questions and answers
- emboldening important information
- increasing the size of some text
- leaving space between lines
- underlining important information

SUCCESSFUL LEAFLETS

Do you want your leaflets to look good?

Then the Successful Leaflets Training Course is for you

Limited places so REGISTER NOW!

Course starts 12 May

25% DISCOUNT for students

For more information contact:
The Leaflet Society, PO Box 24, Leeds LS1 7YH
Freephone 0800 965 965

Issued on 14 March

STAGE 3: IDENTIFY RELEVANT INFORMATION
A leaflet is used to give information about something, eg a sale or a special offer. In every case certain information has to be given. Contact details are essential. This is usually in the form of an address and/or telephone number. It is important that all the information necessary is provided to ensure that whoever reads the leaflet can understand the information and act on it.

STAGE 4: GROUP/ORDER RELEVANT INFORMATION
The information and notes given are often in a suitable order. If the information is not in a suitable order, it is useful to group information and order it in a logical way.

STAGE 5: WRITE THE LEAFLET
The language used in leaflets must be clear and easy to understand. Full sentences are not necessary for the whole text. Slogans may be used if the leaflet is persuading people to buy. Figures, eg 25%, can be used to present information briefly and clearly. Watch out for extra instructions, such as "Be persuasive."

STAGE 6: CHECK YOUR WORK
CHECKLIST: LEAFLETS

1 Have you completed the task? (Will the person who reads the leaflet be able to understand the message?)
2 Is the layout correct?
3 Have you included contact details?
4 Have you included a date of issue?
5 Have you included all the relevant information?
6 Have you ordered the information in the best way?
7 Is the language appropriate for a leaflet?
8 Have you checked spelling, grammar and punctuation?

COMPLETED EXAMPLE

Situation: You work for VIP Pass, a company offering access to over 250 VIP airport lounges worldwide.

Your boss, Mr Richard Crosby, asks you to write a leaflet for him, which can be handed out to passengers in airport departure lounges. He gives you the following information.

VIP Pass offers frequent travellers, especially business travellers, the opportunity to get away from busy airport terminals and to enjoy the peace and tranquillity offered by a VIP lounge. VIP lounges provide the business traveller with everything they are likely to need. Whether they need to phone the office or home, send that important fax or simply surf the internet, VIP Pass makes it possible. Or you can simply enjoy a complimentary light refreshment whilst reading the latest news in one of the many newspapers available free of charge. VIP Pass is so easy to use, where and whenever you find yourself waiting for a flight. For more info and to see for yourself how inexpensive it is visit us at www.vippass.com For your ease and convenience you can even join on-line.

Write the leaflet.

STAGE 1: IDENTIFY THE TASK
Write the leaflet.

STAGE 2: LAYOUT
There are no special rules for layout, however, it must be easy to read, eye-catching and contain contact details and a date.

STAGE 3: IDENTIFY RELEVANT INFORMATION
- VIP Pass
- access to over 250 VIP airport lounges worldwide
- designed specially for business traveller
- escape crowded airports
- peace and quiet
- VIP lounge
- offer telephone/fax/internet access
- complimentary light refreshment
- free newspaper
- simple/convenient/affordable
- for more info
- join on-line

STAGE 4: GROUP/ORDER RELEVANT INFORMATION
1 Luxury of VIP lounges.
2 VIP pass.
3 Escape crowded airports.
4 Relax in peace and quiet.
5 Simple, convenient and affordable.
6 Access to over 250 lounges worldwide.
7 Designed specially for business traveller.
8 Offer telephone, fax and internet access.
9 Free newspaper.
10 Complimentary light refreshment.
11 For more info.
12 Join on-line.

STAGE 5: WRITE THE LEAFLET

ENJOY THE LUXURY OF VIP LOUNGES WORLDWIDE!

With

THE VIP PASS

ESCAPE the chaos of crowded airports
and
RELAX in the peace and quiet of a VIP lounge.

The VIP pass is

SIMPLE, CONVENIENT AND AFFORDABLE

and

gives you

ACCESS TO OVER 250 AIRPORT LOUNGES WORLDWIDE.

Specially designed with the business traveller in mind.

If you need to
TELEPHONE, FAX, access the INTERNET
or simply want to
read the FREE newspaper
and have a COMPLIMENTARY cup of coffee
whilst waiting for your flight, then the VIP pass is for you.

To get more details and to join on-line, visit our website

www.vippass.com

Issued on (today's date)

STAGE 6: CHECK YOUR WORK

CHECKLIST: LEAFLETS

1	Have you completed the task?	✓
2	Is the layout correct?	✓
3	Have you included contact details?	✓
4	Have you included a date of issue?	✓
5	Have you included all the relevant information?	✓
6	Have you ordered the information in the best way?	✓
7	Is the language appropriate for a leaflet?	✓
8	Have you checked spelling, grammar and punctuation?	✓

YOUR EXAMPLE

Situation: Your family run a small picture framing business, Elliot's Art & Framing, at 17 Ashby Road, Headington, Oxford OX2 9BN. Tel: 01865 288 944.

You decide to produce a leaflet to inform customers about all the services your business offers. Here are your notes.

Large number of frames - contemporary & traditional. Picture framing - hand-made frames, all work carried out here in workshop. Experience of all types of artwork: oil paintings/ watercolours/ drawings/ photographs. Also stock certificate frames and ready-made frames. Art materials - broad range of artists' materials - oil paints, watercolour paints, paintbrushes, pencils, sketch boards, paper, card. For kids - fabric paints, face paints, coloured paper, card. Gift vouchers - from £5 upwards. Exhibitions - original paintings/ drawings/ photographs all for sale. No purchase necessary - welcome to browse.

Write the leaflet.

STAGE 1: IDENTIFY THE TASK

....

STAGE 2: LAYOUT

There are no special rules for layout, however, it must be ....,
......................................, and contain .... and ....

STAGE 3: IDENTIFY RELEVANT INFORMATION

....

....

....

....

....

....

....

....

....

....

STAGE 4: GROUP/ORDER RELEVANT INFORMATION

....

....

....

....

....

....

....

....

....

....

STAGE 5: WRITE THE LEAFLET

STAGE 6: CHECK YOUR WORK

CHECKLIST: LEAFLETS

1	Have you completed the task?	
2	Is the layout correct?	
3	Have you included contact details?	
4	Have you included a date of issue?	
5	Have you included all the relevant information?	
6	Have you ordered the information in the best way?	
7	Is the language appropriate for a leaflet?	
8	Have you checked spelling, grammar and punctuation?	

PRACTICE 1

Situation: You work for Harvey Allen Fine Cashmere in their mill shop in Bradford, Yorkshire. The address is 74 New Leeds Road, Bradford, BD14 7AM. Tel: 01274 564 555 Fax: 01274 659 855 Website: www.harveyallen.co.uk

You decide to produce a leaflet, which can be used in Tourist Information Offices throughout Yorkshire, to encourage tourists to visit your mill shop. Use the following article from your local newspaper.

> *At Harvey Allen Fine Cashmere's mill shop at 74 New Leeds Road, 5 miles north of Bradford on A650, you can experience for yourself the luxury of cashmere. You'll find a large range of men's and women's cashmere and lambs wool knitwear in a variety of colours and at prices which compare very favourably with those of their competitors. All the cashmere and knitwear is produced locally in Harvey Allen's own mill. Shopping is made easy for customers who can use any of the major credit cards. For the non-EC visitor there is also the advantage of tax-free shopping. The mill shop is open twelve months of the year, Monday to Friday between 9am and 5pm. Shoppers with cars will find an abundance of free car parking.*
>
> *Bradford Courier (Tuesday)*

Write the leaflet.

PRACTICE 2

Situation: You work for a PR agency. One of your clients is Under the Sea Aquariums Ltd in Blackpool, Lancashire, FY11 8JH, a company who own several aquarium entertainment centres. Tel: 01253 564 888 Website: www.underthesea.co.uk

You are discussing a leaflet with your client. You make the following notes during your meeting.

> **Meeting notes**
>
> **Client:** Under the Sea
> **Date**: 14 March
> **Re**: New Leaflet
>
> Aquarium visit - entertaining, educational, interesting. Over 200 species of fish and other underwater creatures (crabs, starfish, etc). Biggest collection of tiger sharks in Europe. Divers feed fish underwater. State of the art communications system means kids can watch & ask divers questions. Glass tunnel under aquarium (fish all around) - longest tunnel in world - 110m. Large collection of piranhas (meat-eating fish). Also reptile centre (snakes, crocodiles). Online booking/ details of special events on website. Free face-painting. Gift shop & restaurant. Credit/debit cards accepted. Under 16 half-price. Discount for groups of 10+. Opening hours 0930 – 1800 all year. Closed public holidays.

Write the leaflet.

PRACTICE 3

Situation: You work at Monkerston Country House Hotel, Adderston Road, Monkerston, Derbyshire, NH16 5TR. Tel: 01659 7895 9685 Fax: 01659 7894 5612
E-mail: info@monkerstonhouse.co.uk Website: www.monkerstonhouse.co.uk

It is approaching Christmas and the hotel are preparing Christmas cards to send to all of their customers. You work in reception and have just received the following e-mail from your boss, James Dixon, asking you to prepare a leaflet to include in the Christmas card mailing.

Reception

From: James Dixon <j.dixon@monkerstonhouse.co.uk>
To: Reception <reception@monkerstonhouse.co.uk>
Sent: 29 November … 09:30
Subject: Leaflet for Christmas mailing

I want you to produce a leaflet about a special offer we are running in January and February. We'll send the leaflet out with the Christmas cards. The special offer is only available during January and February and is for short breaks. Guests who stay for 3 nights will only be charged for 2 nights. The usual price is £72 per person per night but if guests take advantage of the special offer they will only pay £48 pppn - a saving of £24. The offer doesn't include dinner - only bed & breakfast, but the restaurant will be open for 3, 4 or 5 course dinners in the evening (and, of course, our usual good selection of wines). Mention that all of our rooms have a bathroom and toilet and that we have been awarded 4 stars by the Tourist Board. Don't forget to say that the offer is subject to availability of rooms.

I need the draft by tomorrow lunchtime.

Write the leaflet.

PRACTICE 4

Situation: You work for Eagle Flights, a company which offers balloon flights to corporate and private customers. The company is based at Unit 43, Trafford Industrial Estate, Manchester, MC12 6TG. Freephone: 0990 554 696. E-mail: jan@eagleflights.com Website: www.eagleflights.com

Your boss says, "I want you to produce a leaflet which we can use for mailing. We don't need all the address details, just the freephone number and website. Here are some notes I've made."

Flight of lifetime. Many places throughout country. Flight certificate for all first time fliers. Year-round flights (depending on weather). All pilots have the best qualifications. The most modern equipment. Chance to take photographs through eyes of an eagle. Wide range of flight/gift vouchers. Book in regional office. Also Jan-Mar free photo of you at take-off.

Write the leaflet.

PRACTICE 5

Situation: You work for flygo.com, a budget airline company.

You are preparing a leaflet to be inserted into national Sunday newspapers. Use the notes below.

New year offer. Unbeatable sale now on. 175,000 seats (Jan – Mar). Internet bookings only. Offer exclusive at www.flygo.com. Flights between 10 Jan & 26 Mar. Only on selected flights.

Must stay over a Sat night. London-Belfast £25 return/ London-Edinburgh £30 return/ London-Amsterdam £40 return/ London-Zurich £50 return/ London-Athens £70 return. Fares quoted exclude airport tax. Buy online: www.flygo.com. Take advantage of this offer - must end 24 Nov – midnight. All subject to availability.

Write the leaflet.

PRACTICE 6

Situation: You work for Burrel Insurance Co. Ltd., a company which specialises in competitive insurance policies for people over the age of 50.

Your Office Manager asks you to prepare a leaflet covering details of home, motor, pet and travel insurance for the over 50's. He leaves you this extract from one of your brochures.

We offer large discounts on home insurance for the over 50's. To help customers we have opened a helpline to answer any legal questions and to provide support in case of emergency. The helpline is open 24 hours a day and is free of charge. We can offer as much as 30% additional discount on motor insurance for over 50's, and extra discounts for drivers who don't drive very much. We also have a special agreement with the RAC offering breakdown cover for cars at special rates. With our pet insurance you are covered for vets' fees of up to £500 and we will give you compensation of up to £300 if your pet is stolen or involved in an accident. We provide 3rd party liability of up to £1 million. Our travel insurance is available to everyone, up to any age, and we cover medical expenses up to £2 million. We will give you a free quotation with no obligation on our freephone number 0800 0107 0905.

Write the leaflet.

SECTION 3: NOTICES

STAGE 1: IDENTIFY THE TASK
Read the question and work out exactly what you are required to do. The instruction at the bottom of the question normally reads "Write the notice" or "Draft the notice."

STAGE 2: LAYOUT
A notice requires a clear heading at the top, briefly giving the subject, and an address if appropriate. It must have the name and position of the person who wrote it at the bottom. It must also have a date at the bottom.

IMPORTANT

WHEN WRITING NOTICES YOU MUST

- include a heading
- give the name of the person who wrote it
- give the position of whoever wrote it
- give the date when it was written
- use bullets or numbers if appropriate
- Important information should be in CAPITALS, **bold** or underlined

An address may also be required – so read the question carefully.

Name
Position

Address
Date

STAGE 3: IDENTIFY RELEVANT INFORMATION
A notice is used to inform people about something, eg a change of plan or procedure, a warning or instructions. In every case certain information has to be given. It is essential that all necessary information is provided so that whoever reads the notice can understand the information and act on it.

STAGE 4: GROUP/ORDER RELEVANT INFORMATION
Often the information in the question is presented in a suitable order. Sometimes, however, information is mixed up and repeated or you may have to invent information. After you have identified the relevant information and/or invented information, make sure it is grouped so that points are presented in a logical order.

STAGE 5: WRITE THE NOTICE
The language used in notices must be easy to understand. Full sentences are not always necessary for headings or after bullets but the text requires full sentences.

STAGE 6: CHECK YOUR WORK
CHECKLIST: NOTICES

1 Have you completed the task? (Will the person who reads the notice understand the message?)
2 Is the layout correct?
3 Have you included a date, and a name and position?
4 Have you given the notice a heading?
5 Have you included all the relevant information?
6 Have you ordered the information in the best way?
7 Is the language appropriate for a notice?
8 Have you checked spelling, grammar and punctuation?

COMPLETED EXAMPLE

Situation: You work for Roberts Ltd, a manufacturer of sports clothing, based at Unit 78, Monument Industrial Park, Chalgrove, Oxford OX44 7YB. Tel: 01865 400 987 Fax: 01865 400 555.

The Shop Manager, Mrs Patricia Nelson, asks you to write a notice for her to display the times of factory tours. The notice will be put in the window of the factory shop. Use her notes below.

visit factory - free entry - clothing from start to finish. Times: Jan - Dec.
Mon - Thu 10.30, 11.30, 1.30, 2.30 (or by appointment) Fri (morning only) excl public / local hols.
tour approx 40 mins - specially built factory

Write the notice.

STAGE 1: IDENTIFY THE TASK
Write the notice.

STAGE 2: LAYOUT
A notice requires a clear heading at the top. It must have the name and position of the person who wrote it at the bottom. It must have a date at the bottom.

STAGE 3: IDENTIFY RELEVANT INFORMATION

- Roberts Ltd.
- manufacturers of sports clothing
- Unit 78, Monument Industrial Park, Chalgrove, Oxford OX44 7YB
- Tel: 01865 400 987 Fax: 01865 400 555
- Mrs Patricia Nelson, Shop Manager
- factory tours
- free entry
- production from conception to finished article
- tour times
- Jan - Dec
- Mon - Fri
- 10.30, 11.30, 1.30, 2.30 (or by appointment)
- Fri (morning only)
- excl. public / local hols
- tour lasts approx 40 mins
- purpose built factory

STAGE 4: GROUP/ORDER RELEVANT INFORMATION

1 Roberts Ltd.
2 Manufacturers of sports clothing.
3 Factory Tours.
4 Purpose built factory.
5 Production from conception to finished article.
6 Tour Times.
7 January to December.
8 Monday to Friday.
9 Tours at 10.30 am, 11.30 am, 1.30 pm and 2.30 pm (or by appointment).
10 Friday (morning tours only).
11 Excluding public or local holidays.
12 Tour duration - approximately 40 minutes.
13 Free admission.
14 Mrs Patricia Nelson, Shop Manager.
15 Unit 78, Monument Industrial Park, Chalgrove, Oxford OX44 7YB.
16 Tel: 01865 400 987 Fax: 01865 400 555.
17 Today's date.

STAGE 5: WRITE THE NOTICE

ROBERTS LTD.
Manufacturers of sports clothing

FACTORY TOURS

Conducted tours through our purpose built factory show all aspects of production from conception to the finished article.

Tour Times
January to December
Monday to Friday

Tours at
10.30am, 11.30am, 1.30pm and 2.30pm
(or by appointment)
Friday (morning tours only)

Excluding public or local holidays

Tour duration – approximately 40 minutes.

Free admission

Mrs Patricia Nelson
Shop Manager

Unit 78, Monument Industrial Park, Chalgrove, Oxford OX44 7YB
Tel: 01865 400 987 Fax: 01865 400 555

(today's date)

STAGE 6: CHECK YOUR WORK

CHECKLIST: NOTICES

1	Have you completed the task?	✓
2	Is the layout correct?	✓
3	Have you included a date, and a name and position?	✓
4	Have you given the notice a heading?	✓
5	Have you included all the relevant information?	✓
6	Have you ordered the information in the best way?	✓
7	Is the language appropriate for a notice?	✓
8	Have you checked spelling, grammar and punctuation?	✓

YOUR EXAMPLE

Situation: You work in the Finchley Branch of the National Bank at 334 High Road, Finchley, London, N12 8PL. Tel: 020 4655 6233.

Mrs Edith Knowles, the Branch Manager, says to you, "As you know the Branch will be closing down at the end of June. Write a notice for customers using these notes I've made."

Closing Tue 25 Jun / Apologise inconvenience / to improve efficiency / customers to go to Branch in Hardy Street (directions / location)/ new tel. no.

Write the notice.

STAGE 1: IDENTIFY THE TASK

....

STAGE 2: LAYOUT

A notice requires a clear .... at the top. It must have the ....and .... of the person who wrote it at the bottom. It must have a ....at the bottom.

STAGE 3: IDENTIFY RELEVANT INFORMATION

....

....

....

....

....

....

....

....

....

....

STAGE 4: GROUP/ORDER RELEVANT INFORMATION

....

....

....

....

....

....

....

....

....

....

STAGE 5: WRITE THE NOTICE

STAGE 6: CHECK YOUR WORK

CHECKLIST: NOTICES

1 Have you completed the task?
2 Is the layout correct?
3 Have you included a date, and a name and position?
4 Have you given the notice a heading?
5 Have you included all the relevant information?
6 Have you ordered the information in the best way?
7 Is the language appropriate for a notice?
8 Have you checked spelling, grammar and punctuation?

PRACTICE 1

Setting: You are Office Manager of Blue Star Taxis, 34 King William Street, Aberdeen, AB7 1FG. Tel: 01224 465 988. You are looking for a part-time member of staff to answer the phone in your busy inner-city taxi office. You ask your assistant to draft a notice to put up in the local college. You leave him the following hand-written notes.

> *Immediate start*
> *14 hrs per week* *Flexitime* *Able to work under stress*
> *Pleasant voice* *Friendly & polite*
> *Apply in person* *Ring for appointment.*

Write the notice.

PRACTICE 2

Situation: You work at the Head Office of Como Airlines, Via per Cernobbio 28, Como, Italy. Here is an extract from a recent meeting of the Passenger Service team.

Marco	I think we should **write a notice** that can be placed in our Passenger Lounges to explain to our customers the regulations about luggage on our aircraft.
You	What sort of thing do you mean? Something like 20 kg weight limit?
Marco	Yes, that's right, but 20 kg is for Economy Class only ... Is it 30 kg for First Class?
Manuela	No. First Class is now 40 kg. We made the change in April, and we decided that hand luggage ... you know the bags that passengers can carry with them into the cabin ... would be 5kg maximum.
You	That's for everyone isn't it – First and Economy? Can't they also take some little things ... handbag, coat ... something to read ...?
Manuela	Yes ... as long as they are of a reasonable size ... and, of course, not dangerous.
Marco	The notice should prepare passengers for some of the questions that they will probably be asked ... especially about the luggage. I know I still find it a surprise when some of the questions are asked ... about whether I packed the case myself, for example.
You	Yes. I know the questions have got to be asked, but they are upsetting: "Has your bag been out of your sight?" I'm always worried that it might have been!
Marco	The notice should reassure our passengers that these questions are for their own good – safety, security ...
Manuela	I have just thought. They should take with them any medicine that they might need.

You agree to write the notice.

PRACTICE 3

Situation: You are Information Officer on SS Titania, a ferry operating between Hull, England and Amsterdam, Holland. To welcome passengers aboard and to inform them of what is available on board you decide to draft a notice, which you can put up in all the cabins. Use these notes.

> *Vouchers required for meals - buy from restaurant or Info Office. Hand-in valuables for safekeeping to Info Office. Customer satisfaction is top priority. Unhappy? Report to Info Office. Shopping 1700 - 2300 + 0600 till arrive in port. Change money at Exchange Office. Bars open from sailing. Lounges. Entertainment. Casino open 2000 - 0300. Sunshine lounge - entertainers from 1800 - 0100. Info Office open all time. Recommend lock door if not in or when asleep. Info Office on Blue Deck next to Exchange Office.*

Write the notice.

PRACTICE 4

Setting: You are secretary to Miss Rosie Hill, who is Manager of a Call Centre.

Last week a safety inspector visited the Call Centre. Miss Hill has just received a letter from him in which he advises that on his visit he saw many potential safety risks throughout the Centre. In particular he was critical of staff smoking in areas where they shouldn't have been, eating and drinking at their desks and in general being very careless about closing doors, drawers, cupboards or in putting things away when they were finished with them. He was also concerned that accidents could happen caused by staff running instead of walking. He advised Miss Hill to put up safety notices throughout the Centre.

Task: Write the notice for Miss Hill.

PRACTICE 5

Setting: You work for Mill Street Motors, a new and used Car Sales Centre. Tel: 01522 986 322. The Sales Director is Tom Bowles.

Your boss, Tom Bowles, hands you an email he has just received. He asks you to produce a notice in his name, which can be sent out immediately to all customers, who should call and make an appointment with Maureen Greene to bring their cars in. He asks you to make sure you apologise for any inconvenience.

Tom Bowles

From:	Hank Edwards, C.E.O, Sonopor Car Manufacturers
To:	Tom Bowles, Sales Director, Mill Street Motors
Sent:	13 May
Subject:	URGENT – recall of model ventura sr

Tom

We are going to have to recall all Sonopor Ventura SR's produced between 1st Jan and 1st May (Serial numbers FG121-G19-82369 to FG121-G19-99856). This is due to a fault in the steering column.

Please can you inform all customers. Emphasise that the cars are safe, and that this is just a precautionary measure. Replacement parts are being sent to you and they can be fitted in 2 hours. The situation is regrettable but unavoidable.

Please accept my apologies.

Hank

Write the notice.

PRACTICE 6

Situation: You are Manager of FutureWorldNow Entertainment Park.

The park will open in half an hour's time and you have just been told that one of the new rides, SpaceXpress, is not working. You speak to the engineers who say they have found a fault and recommend that you don't open the ride this morning. You accept their advice and decide to place a notice at the main entrance to inform the public. Use these notes to write the notice.

Safety of public - utmost importance.

Ride closed - this morning - mechanical failure.

Working to fix it
(hopefully by lunchtime).

Apologise inconvenience!

If not fixed today - free tickets.
Customers - ask before leaving.

Write the notice.

STAGE 1: IDENTIFY THE TASK
Write the report.

STAGE 2: LAYOUT
A report requires a title and the following headings:
1 Terms of Reference
2 Proceedings
3 Findings
4 Conclusions
5 Recommendations
It also requires a signature and a date.

STAGE 3: IDENTIFY RELEVANT INFORMATION
- responses to customer satisfaction questionnaires
- report for Mr Sherwood about how satisfied customers are
- to be handed in asap
- 105 cars serviced and questionnaires sent out
- 78 replies received
- were customers satisfied with service?
- 51% are, 39% aren't (no difference)
- are customers satisfied with cost?
- 23% are, 65% aren't (labour and replacement parts)
- are customers satisfied with length of service?
- 25% are, 48% aren't (problem for people not working full-time)
- are customers satisfied with work carried out?
- 62% don't know (not mechanics – how do they know?)
- other comments & suggestions from customers
- showroom unattractive & dark
- suggest free coffee, TV, play area
- general opinions - customers not satisfied
- recommendations - improve planning of services and implement customer suggestions

STAGE 4: GROUP/ORDER RELEVANT INFORMATION
<u>Title</u> Evaluation of Responses to Customer Satisfaction Questionnaire.
<u>Terms of Reference</u> Mr Sherwood has asked for a report on how satisfied customers are with the servicing of their cars. To be completed as soon as possible.
<u>Proceedings</u> Analysed the responses received.
<u>Findings</u>
1 39% were not satisfied. Reasons given: people can't see difference after service. Only 51% satisfied with service.
2 23% were satisfied with the cost of the service. 65% were not satisfied with the cost. Reasons given include that all costs were for labour and customers are charged for replacement parts but they can't check whether they have been replaced or not.
3 48% were not satisfied with the amount of time a service takes. The main problem is that we can't inform them how long the service will last and customers have to wait in the showroom. On one occasion a customer had to wait 4 hours. Only 25% were happy with the length of the service. These were all customers in full-time work, who left the car at the garage all day.
4 62% replied that they didn't know whether they were satisfied with the work carried out. Customers replied that they are not familiar with car engines and how they work.
5 Other comments included that showroom was not very light or clean and not very attractive. Several suggestions for improving facilities in the showroom, eg free coffee, TV, play area for kids.

<u>Conclusions</u>
Customers not satisfied with service and don't like showroom.
<u>Recommendations</u>
Improve planning of service & implement customer suggestions for showroom.

STAGE 5: WRITE THE REPORT

Evaluation of Responses to Customer Satisfaction Questionnaire

Terms of Reference
Mr Sherwood, Managing Director, has asked me to write a report as soon as possible on customer satisfaction regarding the servicing of their cars over the last 3 months.

Proceedings
Of the 105 questionnaires sent out to customers, 78 were returned. I analysed the 78 completed questionnaires, which covered the 5 areas detailed below.

Findings
<u>1 The car service</u>. Over one third (39%) were not happy with the service as there was no obvious improvement in their car's performance. Just over half (51%) were satisfied with the service carried out.

<u>2 The cost</u>. Less than a quarter (23%) were happy with the cost of the service. 65% thought it was too high and complained about the labour charges. There were also questions as to whether replacement parts had been replaced or not.

<u>3 The length of time.</u> Just under half (48%) were dissatisfied with the time taken. In several cases customers had to wait in the showroom as we were unable to say how long a service would take. The 25% who were happy are all in full-time employment and leave the car at the garage all day.

<u>4 The work carried out.</u> The majority of customers replied that they were unable to answer this question because they are not experts in car engine mechanics.

<u>5 Other comments</u>. The general opinion is that our showroom is dark, dirty and unfriendly. Suggestions for improving the facilities included providing free coffee, installing a TV and creating a play area for children.

Conclusions
In general customers are not satisfied with the service we are providing and do not find the showroom very friendly and attractive.

Recommendations
I recommend that we:

1 Plan and timetable services more efficiently and inform customers how long their car service will take.
2 Improve the showroom and make it more customer-friendly by implementing some of the customer suggestions outlined above and by considering redecorating it.

Your name
Date

STAGE 6: CHECK YOUR WORK

CHECKLIST: REPORTS

1	Have you completed the task?	✓
2	Is the layout correct?	✓
3	Does the title tell you briefly what the report is about?	✓
4	Are the headings correct and in the correct order?	✓
5	Have you included the correct information under the correct heading?	✓
6	Have you signed and dated it?	✓
7	Is the language appropriate for a report?	✓
8	Have you checked spelling, grammar and punctuation?	✓

YOUR EXAMPLE

Situation: Mrs Ann Cage is Managing Director of Burger Express, a national chain of fast food restaurants.

Mrs Cage asks you to compile a report about the standard of service at 4 restaurants in the group. She is worried because several complaints have been received recently about these restaurants. You visit the 4 restaurants which are situated in Chester, Shrewsbury, Bristol and Cheltenham and make the following notes.

Re: Standard of Service

Chester

Good, friendly service, helpful staff.
Food served quickly (not very warm!).
Tables clean, staff cleared away used plates quickly.
Staff in general v. young, but seemed adequately trained.

Shrewsbury

V. busy when I was there (Sat. morning).
Restaurant full, queues outside door, no seating available.
Staff managing well.
Problem was customers not leaving when finished meal, sitting talking at tables.
Many customers in queue complaining about waiting time.

Bristol

As with Shrewsbury - queues outside door.
Different reasons:
- *service slow*
- *seats available but tables piled high with used plates.*

Only 1 employee clearing tables.
Told many staff hadn't turned in that day (often happened).
Customers had to clear own tables.

Cheltenham

Similar to Chester - good service, food served quickly.
BUT burgers not cooked long enough, no onions, cheese tasted like leather.
In kitchen youngsters doing cooking - appeared to have no idea.

Write the report.

STAGE 1: IDENTIFY THE TASK

....

STAGE 2: LAYOUT

A report requires a .... and the following headings: 1...
2.. 3.. 4...
5.. It also requires a .... and a ....

STAGE 3: IDENTIFY RELEVANT INFORMATION

....
....
....
....
....
....
....
....
....
....
....
....
....
....
....
....

STAGE 4: GROUP/ORDER RELEVANT INFORMATION

....
....
....
....
....
....
....
....
....
....
....
....
....
....
....

Situation: AG Gold Co. is an international chain of jewellery shops. You are Shop Manager of the AG Shop in Edinburgh's Waverley Shopping Centre.

Over the last 6 months the shop's profits have fallen dramatically. The Regional Manager, Andrew Sheringham, has asked you to write a report on the reasons for the decrease in sales. Here are some notes you have made.

1. Strong pound
   Fewer foreign tourists to Edinburgh
   Sales of Celtic design down (popular with Europeans)
   40% fewer American tourists this year
   - Americans can buy tax-free
   - 15% of shop turnover last year from American tourists

2. Shops left and right closed down
   Bad impression
   Makes shop isolated, people walk past

3. Shoplifting by school children (particularly girls age 14 – 17)
   Major increase in this over last 6 months
   Come in groups of around 10, can't keep an eye on all of them
   Costs shop a lot!
   Install camera?

4. Customers asking for a sale or discount
   Go to other jewellery shops that have sales on
   Company policy 'no sales, no discount'

Write the report.

Situation: There has been much talk recently about the proposed merger of the UK company Pylo Plastics with the US company Penn Plastics Inc. The Board of Directors of the UK company want to find out how their employees would feel about such a merger. They ask you, the Personnel Manager, to find out and to produce your findings in the form of a report. You speak to all Department Heads individually and to staff in groups during lunchbreaks in the staff canteen. These are the notes you make.

Staff in particular not clear whether merger or takeover.
Heads of Depts clearer on this point but not clear exactly how merger could work.
Nobody clear as to effects of merger.
Will there be job losses?
Voluntary redundancies?
Even factory closure?
Transfer to other sites in UK (Penn Plastics Inc already has 2 UK factories)?
Will management stay or be changed?
Head Office here or in US?
Will staff be consulted before merger or is it foregone conclusion?

Write the report.

STAGE 6: CHECK YOUR WORK

CHECKLIST: REPORTS

1 Have you completed the task? ☐
2 Is the layout correct? ☐
3 Does the title tell you briefly what the report is about? ☐
4 Are the headings correct and in the correct order? ☐
5 Have you included the correct information under the correct heading? ☐
6 Have you signed and dated it? ☐
7 Is the language appropriate for a report? ☐
8 Have you checked spelling, grammar and punctuation? ☐

PRACTICE 3

Situation: You are Sales Manager of the Worldwide Music Company (WMC), South Bank, London, SE1 8XC.

You have just returned from a sales conference and your Sales Director, Mr Gary Hayes, says, "That's the first time the company has used Roundtree Conference Centre. Let me have a report on the suitability of it for future conferences or training seminars." Use your notes.

2 sources of information: own impressions and talked to staff during conference.

4 main areas:
***Accommodation rooms -** tea/coffee making facilities, TV, air-conditioned, en suite bath or shower. Some staff said rooms not very big, but size was adequate.*

***Conference rooms -** Centre has 4 conference rooms (for 20, 40, 60 and 100 people).*
Used the 'Highgrove Room' – ideal for 35 participants at conference.
Layout – tables arranged in U-shape, very effective. Many arrangement possibilities – lots of flexibility. Equipment all worked (OHP, Laptop presentation). Lots of windows - very light in room.
Seats - not very comfortable after 2 hours! (not helpful when I mentioned this).
Acoustics - good. Sat at back, could hear every word.

***Food -** very good, lots of variety (also offer healthy choice).*

***Relaxation Centre -** well-equipped but very busy early evening. Swimming pool - very small.*

Write the report.

PRACTICE 4

Situation: You are Sales Manager of Mercury plc, a large electronics company.

Your Personnel Department recently sent you two young men who were interested in a full-time job in sales. It was agreed to give them a one-month trial at the end of which one of the men would be offered a full-time position. Your company's Personnel Manager, Ms Katy Dixon, will make this decision but she asks you for your opinion in the form of a report. Use the notes you have kept.

Jake Sinclair and Barry Brewster

Started work in sales on Mon 3 Sept.

Both work directly under my supervision.

JS & BB have been on time every day.

Always ready to start at 9 and willing to stay on after 5pm if required.

Both well-dressed, get on well with colleagues.

J more outgoing (18 months older) than B – most obvious when talking to customers or telephoning. B more reserved, chooses words more carefully. If he can't answer a customer's question he'll say so and find out answer. J will talk & talk.

Write the report.

PRACTICE 5

Situation: You are Chief Safety Officer at Cosmos Transport plc.

Over the past 6 months there have been a number of minor accidents in your Central Warehouse in Exeter. Last week an employee was badly injured when a fork-lift truck reversed into him. Your MD, Sir Humphrey McAulay, has instructed you to go to Exeter and compile a report about this accident with recommendations as to how the safety record in the warehouse can be improved. You use the accident report card below and speak to staff who were present at the time. Here are your notes.

<u>Conversation with Arthur Smedley</u>

At time of accident Arthur Smedley working with Wilfred Smith.

AS said both hurrying to get finished (should have been finished at 18.00). More a case of WS walking into fork-lift truck rather than F-LT backing into WS. (WS had been hurrying down the passage and turned into passage just as F-LT was backing out). Driver had no chance to stop.

<u>Conversation with Warehouse Manager</u>

Warehouse Manager confirmed all staff working overtime because 4 workers off ill. All employees working in warehouse are new, none with company for more than 6 weeks. Not yet received any safety training - no time. Staff turnover high, job poorly paid.

<u>ACCIDENT REPORT CARD</u>

Name of injured person:	Wilfred Smith
Position:	Warehouse Assistant
Date of accident:	14 April
Time of accident:	18.45

What happened?

A fork-lift truck which was driven by Henry Stevens reversed into Wilfred Smith in passage 3b of the warehouse.

Action taken:

An ambulance was called at 18.48. WS was taken to the Casualty Department of Exeter General Hospital. His right leg was broken in two places.

Write the report.

PRACTICE 6

Situation: You are an Administrative Assistant in the Finance Department of Paul Kavanagh Distribution Ltd.

Last week Mrs Gerard, the Financial Director, called you into her office and asked you to write a report on the increase in the amount of paper being used. You have done some research into the problem and made the following notes. Use the notes to write the report.

Checked with accounts
- paper orders (and costs!) have tripled over 6 months!!!

Reasons for this? Spoke to staff & management.

1 Increase in e-mails sent/ received
Some messages several pages long (especially replied messages/ forwarded messages). Some messages very short (eg "thanks"). Staff print out every message, irrespective of how long it is.

2 Faster printers
Very easy and quick to print - employees don't check work on screen (careless) - they print out, then correct and print again - documents often printed up to 4 times before final version - most thrown into wastepaper bin.

3 Print out web pages
Many employees now finding information through internet. Find useful web page and print it, then find another and print it, etc. Later thrown away.

4 Print documents every time they are needed
Particularly young staff (lazy) - don't like filing, don't like looking for documents. Easier and faster to print out again.

Write the report.

SECTION 5: ARTICLES

STAGE 1: IDENTIFY THE TASK
Read the question and work out exactly what you are required to do. The instruction at the bottom of the question normally reads "Write the article." It is useful to note down any additional instructions, eg "Add any other information you think may be useful."

STAGE 2: LAYOUT
An article requires an underlined title and should consist of several paragraphs. The text should have:

- an arresting opening
- a middle
- a closing sentence or paragraph.

Below is an example of layout for an article.

<u>**Writing an Article**</u>

How do you make the opening of an article interesting? One way is to start the first paragraph with a question and then provide an answer.

If you want to make the reader read on, you have to make it interesting and direct the text at the reader. One way is to use 'you' in the article.

Before you start, however, you should always read the question carefully and work out exactly what you are required to do. Think about what the article is for - is it for a company newsletter or a magazine? Then work out who the intended reader of the article is and decide what information is useful and important.

When you write the article divide the text into several paragraphs. Each paragraph should have a theme and they should be in a logical order.

After you have written the article, remember to check your work properly and don't forget to make up information if you are required to do so.

So, now you know how to write an article – what are you waiting for?

STAGE 3: IDENTIFY RELEVANT INFORMATION
An article is written to give information to the reader. Read the question and decide what information is important to the reader in order to complete the task. You are often asked to invent information. Again, decide what information is useful and important to the reader and make it up accordingly.

STAGE 4: GROUP/ORDER RELEVANT INFORMATION
The first paragraph should make the reader want to read on. All the points you want to make should follow in a logical order and they should be drawn together or concluded in the final paragraph.

STAGE 5: WRITE THE ARTICLE
Articles are usually written to go into a magazine (eg company magazine or newsletter). They should be narrative and informative. Watch out for extra instructions, eg questions which say, "Your article should be interesting and persuasive" or "Add anything else you think is relevant."

STAGE 6: CHECK YOUR WORK
CHECKLIST: ARTICLES

1 Have you completed the task?
2 Is the layout correct?
3 Is the title suitable?
4 Does it have an opening, a middle and an ending?
5 Have you included all the relevant information?
6 Have you ordered the information in the best way?
7 Is the language appropriate for an article?
8 Have you checked spelling, grammar and punctuation?

COMPLETED EXAMPLE

Situation: You work for CPI international airlines.

You company has recently installed a new self-service check-in system called 'Check & Go'. Your boss asks you to write an article for your airline's passenger magazine explaining the new system and encouraging people to use it. Here are your notes.

'Check & Go' – new time-saving idea
Check in automatically and get boarding card
- no queue
How it works: Put ticket into machine
Flight details are shown on screen
Check details are correct & press 'confirm' button
Answer usual questions about luggage, passport, etc
Available seats appear on screen, select seat & press 'confirm'
Boarding pass printed
Go straight to gate
'C&G' computer terminals installed in all UK airports
Only for passengers with pre-paid ticket & hand-luggage

Write the article.

STAGE 1: IDENTIFY THE TASK
Write the article.

STAGE 2: LAYOUT
An article requires a title, an interesting opening, a middle and an ending.

STAGE 3: IDENTIFY RELEVANT INFORMATION
- CPI international airlines 'Check & Go'
- new time-saving idea
- check in automatically & obtain boarding card
- no queue
- insert ticket into machine
- flight details are shown on screen
- check details are correct & press 'confirm' button
- answer usual questions about luggage, passport, etc
- available seats appear on screen, choose seat & press 'confirm'
- boarding pass printed
- passengers can go straight to gate.
- 'C&G' computer terminals in all UK airports
- only passengers with pre-paid ticket & hand-luggage

STAGE 4: GROUP/ORDER RELEVANT INFORMATION
1 'Check & Go' self-service check-in from CPI international airlines.
2 Only passengers with a pre-paid ticket and hand-luggage.
3 Check in automatically and obtain boarding pass.
4 No queue.
5 Passengers insert ticket into the machine.
6 Flight details appear on the screen.
7 Check details are correct and press "confirm" button.
8 Usual questions about hand-luggage, passport etc.
9 Available seats appear on screen.
10 Choose a seat and press "confirm" button.
11 Boarding pass printed.
12 Passengers can go straight to gate.
13 Computer terminals in all UK airports.
14 Time-saving idea.

STAGE 5: WRITE THE ARTICLE

CHECK & GO SELF-SERVICE CHECK-IN

Tired of standing in those endless check-in queues? Then try the new Check & Go self-service check-in from CPI international airlines.

If you have a pre-paid ticket and only have hand-luggage, you can check yourself in automatically and obtain a boarding pass for your flight without having to queue.

All you have to do is follow the on-screen instructions. You are asked to insert your ticket into the machine after which your flight details appear on the screen. Once you have checked these details, you press the "confirm" button. You will then be asked all the standard questions about your hand-luggage, passport and any visa requirements there may be.

At this stage all seats that are available on the flight are displayed on a diagram of the aircraft. You can choose where you would like to sit by selecting the seat and pressing the "confirm" button.

Finally, your boarding pass is printed and you can go straight to your departure gate.

Check & Go computer terminals have now been installed in all UK airports, so it doesn't matter which airport you are flying from.

If you haven't tried it yet you're missing out on one of the best time-saving ideas around.

STAGE 6: CHECK YOUR WORK

CHECKLIST: ARTICLES

1	Have you completed the task?	✓
2	Is the layout correct?	✓
3	Is the title suitable?	✓
4	Does it have an opening, a middle and an ending?	✓
5	Have you included all the relevant information?	✓
6	Have you ordered the information in the best way?	✓
7	Is the language appropriate for an article?	✓
8	Have you checked spelling, grammar and punctuation?	✓

YOUR EXAMPLE

Situation: You work for AEC Hydroelectric plc.

A year ago your company built a new Visitor Centre. Your boss gives you the following notes to write an article for a magazine produced by the National Tourist Office. The article should provide information about the company and its centre.

AEC founded 1989.
Provides electricity to over 500,000 homes and businesses.
Visitor centre - opened last June, more than 30,000 visitors.
Open 7 days, 10 - 8pm. Closed bank holidays. Free entry.
Exhibitions & displays.
Just the thing for children, school parties, family days out.
- 'Moving Water' exhibition / Model of power station / 'Power of Water' display, etc.
Centre has won many awards for design (The New Building Award from the CBI).
- "Very important architectural project" (Daily News).
- "Very entertaining and educational" (Morning Star).
- "The exhibitions were simply fascinating" (The Courier).

Write the article.

STAGE 1: IDENTIFY THE TASK

....

STAGE 2: LAYOUT

An article requires a ...., an interesting..,
a .... and an ....

STAGE 3: IDENTIFY RELEVANT INFORMATION

....
....
....
....
....
....
....
....
....
....

STAGE 4: GROUP/ORDER RELEVANT INFORMATION

....
....
....
....
....
....
....
....
....
....

STAGE 5: WRITE THE ARTICLE

STAGE 6: CHECK YOUR WORK

CHECKLIST: ARTICLES

1	Have you completed the task?	
2	Is the layout correct?	
3	Is the title suitable?	
4	Does it have an opening, a middle and an ending?	
5	Have you included all the relevant information?	
6	Have you ordered the information in the best way?	
7	Is the language appropriate for an article?	
8	Have you checked spelling, grammar and punctuation?	

PRACTICE 1

Situation: You work for VTR, a UK car manufacturing company. Your company is planning to expand into Spain and your boss has just returned from a successful business trip to Barcelona. He hands you some notes and says, "The trip to Spain was very interesting. Hopefully we'll be sending one or two employees out in the next few months. There are a few things that they need to know before they go. Use my notes to write an article for the next newsletter."

Spain:- Working hours: 9.30 - 13.30 & 16.30 - 20.30 'Siesta' 13.30 - 16.30.
Work - no special norms, but light clothes (hot!) - recommend lightweight suit, short-sleeved shirt & tie. Evenings: informal dress - recommend smart/casual.
Restaurants no fixed opening hours. Bars early till late.
Tipping - great tradition. In restaurants/cafes often included, normal to leave extra tip (5-10%) also taxi drivers.
Banks 08.30 – 14.30. Mon – Sat. Closed Sun. Also closed Sat in summer .

Write the article.

PRACTICE 2

Situation: You work for DIDA Educational Publishing House, which is based in Prague, Czech Republic. You are preparing information for an international book fair that your company is attending. Your boss, Mrs Silanova, has asked you to write an article for the exhibition magazine which will be given free to all visitors. She gives you the following notes.

Established Prague 1993. Publisher of educational books.
Specialisation – school textbooks / teachers' resource materials / students' self-study workbooks. Own retail outlets in 30 towns & cities in CR. Print under licence.
Distribute for foreign publishers in Czech Republic. Supply other bookshops in CR.
1996 started sister company – Poland.
Same services – publishing, distribution, printing under licence. Extra benefit for foreign publishers that 2 markets covered by one distributor. Don't forget to mention stand number & who's on stand. Add any other information you think may be useful.

Write the article.

PRACTICE 3

Situation: You work for Glasden Chemicals. Your boss says to you, "Rita Powell has worked for the company for 40 years. I think we should put an article in the company magazine about this congratulating her and thanking her for her loyalty. Can you write it for me? Here are some notes I made at her presentation yesterday."

Rita Powell - left school 16 & joined G.C. - Never left. Now works in Wages Dept.
Lived through 40 years of changes – everything by hand then, now computers - Rita, "This has kept it interesting." Presentation in factory with colleagues past & present. Gold clock plus gifts.

Write the article.

PRACTICE 4

Situation: You work for MultiPrint. The Managing Director is Mr Chris Thompson.

Mr Thompson asks you to write an article for the company magazine about last Friday's official opening of the company's new head office at Ringway House. Here are his notes.

Official opening – Ringway House – Fri 27 Apr. Thank staff – great day.
Stage in main hall – company's colours – multi-screen powerpoint display – company's work.
Distinguished business visitors. Chairman (Bill Shed) official welcome.
Guided tour – latest printing technology in use. Visitors impressed – opening in working factory.

Add any other information you think may be useful.

Write the article.

PRACTICE 5

Situation: You are a student of International Management in London. Last year you spent a year at le Faculte des Sciences Economiques in Geneva, Switzerland. Your year was funded by DGFT Consulting, an international management consultancy company.

DGFT have asked you to write an article for their in-house magazine about your year abroad. The article should provide information about what you gained from your experience and how the year has helped prepare you for a future in international management. Here are your notes.

Course requirement to spend 1 year abroad - studying.
Before left felt like 1st year student again - new friends / city / uni / country.
School French! - Often been to Switzerland.
IM course v. good/ studied int. management / marketing / export.
Now: French excellent - tremendous experience - really grateful - able to really understand diff. culture.

Write the article.

PRACTICE 6

Situation: You are Training Officer at Wills Electronics.

Your company has a very good record of investing in employee development. Write an article for your company's in-house magazine. Here are your notes.

Employee development - top priority. Employees at all levels benefit. Currently 350 staff on training / language courses. Invested £7 mil+ in training & development last year. 250 trainees aged under 18 have special 2 year programme. Aim: to learn key aspects of job. Also gain accredited qualification. Graduate programme - recruiting for management. Work placement for apprentice engineers.

Write the article. Add any other information you think may be useful.

SECTION 6: LISTS

STAGE 1: IDENTIFY THE TASK
Read the question and work out exactly what you are required to do and what the list is to be used for. The instruction at the bottom of the question normally reads "Write the list."

STAGE 2: LAYOUT
A list should have a title and numbered points. Sub-headings can be used and should be emboldened or underlined. Two examples of layout for lists are shown below:

TITLE OF LIST

1 **First Heading**
- point 1
- point 2

2 **Second Heading**

Sub-heading 1
- point 1
- point 2
- point 3

Sub-heading 2
- point 1
- point 2

3 **Third Heading**
- point 1
- point 2

TITLE OF LIST

1 Write the first point on your list.

2 Write the next point on your list.

3 Write the next point on your list.

4 Write the next point on your list.

5 Write the next point on your list.

6 Write the next point on your list.

7 Write the final point on your list.

STAGE 3: IDENTIFY RELEVANT INFORMATION
Read the question and decide what information should be included in the list. It should be enough so that nothing essential is left out.

STAGE 4: GROUP/ORDER RELEVANT INFORMATION
The information given is often in a suitable order. If it is mixed up or repeated, make sure information concerning the same theme is grouped together.

STAGE 5: WRITE THE LIST
The language used in lists is to the point. It is often for someone to refer to at a meeting so should be brief but contain all the information, so that the reader can talk from it.

STAGE 6: CHECK YOUR WORK
CHECKLIST: LISTS
1 Have you completed the task? (Will the person who has to read it have all the information necessary?)
2 Is the layout correct?
3 Have you given the list a title?
4 Have you used numbered points and headings if appropriate?
5 Have you included all the relevant information?
6 Have you ordered the information in the best way?
7 Is the language appropriate for a list?
8 Have you checked spelling, grammar and punctuation?

COMPLETED EXAMPLE

Situation: You work for Hearnsey Castle Gardens Ltd.

This evening you are going to give a talk to a group of visiting French tourists. Use the information below and make a list to refer to during your talk.

Hearnsey Castle Gardens are situated two and a half miles from the town centre on the B3258 road. The gardens are open 7 days a week throughout the year. Bookings from organised groups are welcome.

During the summer months, which is from the end of March to the end of October, the gardens are open from 11am – 5.30pm, and visitors can enjoy the Walled and Wild Gardens, Woodland Walks, Restaurant, other attractions and events. Season tickets are available during the summer season. In the winter months, from the end of October to March, visitors can enjoy the Walled and Wild Gardens and Woodland Walks during daylight hours.

The large Domestic Garden is on a grand scale and lies at the centre of this traditional estate occupying a beautiful position on the River Severn. The garden is surrounded by magnificent hills and planted with a wide variety of mature specimen trees. Within the Walled Garden are greenhouses, which house many unusual species of plants, and an enchanting rose garden. The 12 acres of Wild Garden feature Woodland and Riverside Walks and provides a rich variety of colour and charm for both the keen gardener, or for the visitor simply wanting to enjoy a beautiful garden in peaceful surroundings.

Other attractions include a Gift Shop, Children's Corner, Art Gallery and Tearoom/Restaurant. The Art Gallery is situated in the courtyard opposite the Restaurant and has regular exhibitions of invited artists throughout the summer. The Tearoom/Restaurant serves morning coffee, lunches and afternoon teas, 11am – 5.30pm. Bookings for lunch are advisable. Coach parties and evening parties can be admitted by arrangement. Special events are held throughout the summer. Information can be obtained from the estate office or from the local press.

During the summer months the admission charge is £2 for adults and 50p for children (aged between 5 and 14). During the winter months the charge is £1 for adults and 50p for children (5 – 14). There is no charge for children under 5.

Hearnsey is not a National Trust garden, but is privately owned and run by the Hearnsey family.

We hope you will enjoy it with us.

Write the list.

STAGE 1: IDENTIFY THE TASK
Write the list.

STAGE 2: LAYOUT
A list requires a title and numbered points.

STAGE 3: IDENTIFY RELEVANT INFORMATION

- located 2.5 miles from town centre on B3258
- gardens open 7 days a week all year
- bookings from organised groups welcome
- summer season opening
  - end Mar - end-Oct (11 - 5.30)
  - walled gardens, wild gardens, woodland walks, restaurant, other attractions and events
  - season tickets available
- winter season opening
  - end Oct - Mar (daylight hours)
  - walled & wild gardens and woodland walks
- domestic garden
  - large, grand scale at centre of estate
  - beautiful position on River Severn
  - surrounded by magnificent hills
  - wide variety of mature specimen trees
- walled garden
  - greenhouses
  - many unusual species of plants
  - rose garden (enchanting)
- wild garden
  - 12 acres
  - woodland and riverside walks
  - provide a variety of colour and charm for keen gardener
  - beautiful garden in peaceful surroundings for visitor
- other attractions
  Gift Shop
  Children's Corner
  Art Gallery
  - regular exhibitions through summer
  Tearoom/Restaurant
  - morning coffee, lunches and afternoon teas (11 - 5.30)
  - bookings for lunch advisable
  - coach parties / evening parties by arrangement
- general
  - special events held throughout the summer
  - information from estate office or local press
- prices
  Summer: £2 / Children (5 – 14) 50p / Under 5 free
  Winter: £1 / Children (5 – 14) 50p / Under 5 free
- Hearnsey not a National Trust garden, but privately owned and run by the family

STAGE 4: GROUP/ORDER RELEVANT INFORMATION

1 Location
2 Gardens
- Domestic Garden
- Walled Garden
- Wild Garden

3 Other attractions
- Art Gallery
- Tearoom/Restaurant

4 Opening times
- Summer season
- Winter season

5 General
6 Prices

STAGE 5: WRITE THE LIST

HEARNSEY CASTLE GARDENS LTD.

1 Location 2.5 miles from town centre on B3258

2 Gardens

Domestic Garden
- large, grand scale
- beautiful position on River Severn
- surrounded by magnificent hills
- wide variety of mature specimen trees

Walled Garden
- greenhouses with many unusual plant species
- enchanting rose garden

Wild Garden
- 12 acres
- Woodland and Riverside Walks
- variety of colour/charm for keen gardener
- beautiful garden in peaceful surroundings for visitors

3 Other attractions

Gift Shop
Children's Corner

Art Gallery
- regular exhibitions throughout summer

Tearoom/Restaurant (11 - 5)
- morning coffee, lunches and afternoon teas
- bookings for lunch advisable
- coach parties / evening parties by arrangement

4 Opening times
- gardens open 7 days a week all year
- bookings from organised groups welcome

Summer season (end March - end-October)
- 11am – 5.30pm
- Walled and Wild Gardens, Woodland Walks,
- Restaurant, other attractions and events
- Season tickets available

Winter season (end October - March)
- daylight hours
- Walled & Wild Gardens and Woodland Walks

5 General
- special events held throughout the summer
- information from the office or from the local press
- Hearnsey not a National Trust garden
- privately owned and run by the family

6 Prices

• Summer:	Adults £2	Children (5 – 14) 50p	Under 5's free
• Winter:	Adults £1	Children (5 – 14) 50p	Under 5's free

STAGE 6: CHECK YOUR WORK

CHECKLIST: LISTS

1	Have you completed the task?	✓
2	Is the layout correct?	✓
3	Have you given the list a title?	✓
4	Have you used numbered points and headings if appropriate?	✓
5	Have you included all the relevant information?	✓
6	Have you ordered the information in the best way?	✓
7	Is the language appropriate for a list?	✓
8	Have you checked spelling, grammar and punctuation?	✓

YOUR EXAMPLE

Situation: You work for Mrs Carol Young, who owns a lot of property. You are responsible for the administration of the flats she rents out.

Last week you installed a new washer dryer in the basement of one of Mrs Young's blocks of flats, after the last one broke down. There are 10 flats in the block, all of which share the washing machine. Use the information from the user's manual below and make a list of DO'S and DONT'S to hang on the wall above the machine.

USER'S MANUAL

This machine should only be used for its intended purpose as described in the manual which should be fully understood before operating. This machine includes many safety features including a door interlock, which prevents the door being opened when there is water in the drum or if the drum is still turning. If for some reason the door will not open wait a moment or two and try again. Do not try to force it.

Garments treated with flammable cleaning sprays or liquids, such as petrol, must not be put in this machine. As with all washing machines, coins or similar small metal objects can damage the drum. The manufacturers will not accept responsibility for damage caused by such items.

Heavy items such as bath mats, cotton sheets and towels should not be washed on their own but should be washed as part of a well balanced load.

If you use dispensing devices for concentrated washing powder and liquid detergent then they must be removed from the drum before tumble drying. All foam and rubber articles are not suitable for tumble drying and must not be placed in the dryer.

During tumble drying the drum inside the washing machine may get very hot. In the interests of safety always allow the dryer to complete the cool down period before removing your washing. When tumble drying it is imperative that the cold water supply is turned on.

If the machine appears to be faulty do not continue to use it. After use always make sure that you turn off the water supplies and remove the plug from the electricity supply.

Write the list.

STAGE 1: IDENTIFY THE TASK

....

STAGE 2: LAYOUT

A list requires a .... and ....

STAGE 3: IDENTIFY RELEVANT INFORMATION

....

....

....

....

....

....

....

....

....

....

....

....

....

....

....

....

....

....

....

....

....

STAGE 4: GROUP/ORDER RELEVANT INFORMATION

....

....

....

....

....

....

....

....

....

....

....

STAGE 5: WRITE THE LIST

STAGE 6: CHECK YOUR WORK

CHECKLIST: LISTS

1	Have you completed the task?	
2	Is the layout correct?	
3	Have you given the list a title?	
4	Have you used numbered points and headings if appropriate?	
5	Have you included all the relevant information?	
6	Have you ordered the information in the best way?	
7	Is the language appropriate for a list?	
8	Have you checked spelling, grammar and punctuation?	

PRACTICE 1

Situation: You work for Domestic Appliances Ltd, a company, which manufactures DAL fire extinguishers.

You have been asked to give a talk on fire prevention and fire safety to a group of business people in your local town. List the important details from the information below to refer to during your talk.

All our fire extinguishers are manufactured to a high specification providing excellent fire protection with assured performance. They are designed to be refilled when necessary and are fitted with a pressure gauge, indicating serviceability at a glance. It is important when you first purchase a fire extinguisher that you read the operating instructions carefully, so that you are familiar with how to use it because in the stress of a fire emergency, you may not have time to familiarise yourself. When installing a fire extinguisher in the home install it where it can be easily seen and reached in the event of a fire starting. Recommended installation areas include the hallway or on a landing or in the kitchen. It may even be appropriate to have an extinguisher on each floor. If you are fitting your extinguisher into a motor vehicle it must be positioned so that it is immediately accessible to the occupants of the vehicle at all times, consequently do not place it in the boot or any other location where access is restricted. It is important that all extinguishers are firmly fixed otherwise they could cause injury during a car accident. In the event of a fire our advice is to stop the vehicle in the safest position possible and to turn off the ignition. Get out of the vehicle and call the Fire Brigade immediately. Deal with the fire with your extinguisher only if it is safe to do so. If it is too intense, stand well back and leave it to the Fire Brigade. If the fire is in the engine compartment do not open the bonnet fully as a sudden rush of air will increase the size of the fire. If possible open the bonnet on its safety catch and point the extinguisher through the gap. The British Standard recommendation is that each extinguisher should be properly inspected annually.

Write the list.

PRACTICE 2

Situation: You work for the organisers of LinguaMarkt, an international language fair held every year.

You have been invited to give a talk at a local training college to inform teachers and students about the fair and encourage them to attend. Make a list of the main points from this article to use as a hand-out during your talk.

This year's 10th LinguaMarkt Stuttgart, Germany's largest international Language Fair, has as its main theme the future language requirements of European business. Learning other languages has become a responsibility for future generations, a prerequisite for peaceful cooperation between nations as well as a necessity in increasingly global markets.

Learning other languages is no longer an option. We owe it not only to ourselves and our careers but to the successful future of our children. A knowledge of at least one other language can no longer be regarded as an additional skill, it is an essential skill for many careers and jobs. Because during your school days you can only learn so much, language learning has become a life-long obligation.

More than 200 exhibitors from 30 countries will present their programmes and services at this year's fair. Services and products on offer range from language courses and travel to language related teaching materials, software and multimedia products, literature, dictionaries, qualifications and examining bodies. This year LinguaMarkt Stuttgart will take place in a new venue, the Stuttgart Conference and Exhibition Centre, which can easily be reached from the city centre by public transport.

Write the list.

PRACTICE 3

Situation: You are Assistant Manager of a shop, which sells electrical goods.

Your boss gives you the information below and says "Here's some information about the new ELEC Fridge Freezer. Make a list of the main points for the sales staff to refer to."

When choosing an ELEC Fridge Freezer you can be sure that you are getting the best in advanced cooling and freezing technology in your own kitchen. All ELEC Fridge Freezers incorporate the latest product innovations to ensure that your food is stored safely. Specially designed doors offer a covered dairy compartment to ensure dairy foods don't pick up flavours from other items in the fridge, plus many models have a butter dish and egg trays. Glass shelves provide a stable nonslip surface and help to ensure that there is no cross contamination of foods. A tall bottle flap that allows for storage of large bottles upright and a tilting upper shelf keeps corks wet when chilling wine. Both fresh meat and salad can be stored hygienically in the meat/salad box. The unique reversible lid seals for storing salad, or allows ventilation essential when storing fresh meat. The salad compartments consist of sturdy plastic drawers and include a specialised two drawer fruit and vegetable store providing sufficient space for keeping fresh produce in bulk. In the freezer a special construction at the front of the shelves and baskets prevents cold air escaping when you open the door. There's a special holder on the door for a freezer storage card which provides a check on food stock as well as useful advice on home freezing. ELEC Fridge Freezers are designed with simplicity of use in mind. Easy to operate control panels incorporate a fast freeze switch and a temperature warning light. All ELEC Fridge Freezers have two compressors, allowing independent thermostat control for the fridge and freezer compartments.

Write the list.

PRACTICE 4

Situation: You work for Sunshine Insurance and specialise in personal travel insurance.

You have decided to draw up a list of the main points from this article, which you can give to all your company's reps to help them when selling travel insurance to customers.

According to new research travel agents and tour operators are still the major providers of travel insurance, but nearly one in six travellers now buy direct from an insurance company. Research has shown that as consumers have become more knowledgeable about the intricacies of travel insurance and the various types of cover on offer, they are beginning to demand lower prices and higher levels of service. The research has revealed that insurance premiums can vary by as much as 50% for the same level of cover. There are a number of key features, which should be included in any holiday insurance cover. It is important that you are insured against cancellation of your holiday, and medical cover should be at least £1m for travel within Europe and double that if you are heading further afield. Adequate personal liability insurance is essential, especially if you are travelling to the United States where the cost of a lawsuit could bankrupt you. You may even be refused entry into the US unless you have at least £2 million public liability cover. You should also ensure that there is sufficient cover for lost, stolen or damaged baggage as well as for "first needs" while waiting for your luggage to catch up with you. Some holiday insurance companies exclude cover for money, valuables and baggage so as to keep the premium down but if your valuables are stolen you would need to claim on your home contents insurance. As with all other areas of insurance, shopping around pays off. Research has also shown that annual travel insurance is becoming very popular as people take more frequent trips abroad. In the last two years the number of customers choosing annual travel insurance has increased five-fold.

Write the list.

PRACTICE 5

Setting: You are an Administrative Assistant in a medical practice. One of the Doctors gives you the article below and says, "I'm giving a talk at a conference next week. Here's an article I wrote for a medical journal last month. Can you make a list of the major points which I can use as an overhead during my talk?"

> The number of overweight people worldwide has now caught up with the number of people who are underfed according to statistics from a US based research organisation. There are 1.2 billion overfed or obese adults, equal to the number who have too little to eat. Poor countries are piling on the pounds, along with Western Europe, as populations move away from the country to a more sedentary city life.
>
> In Britain about half of all adults are now too fat, and obesity rates have doubled in a decade. Latin American countries are rapidly catching up. In Brazil, 31% of the population are overweight, and in Columbia the figure is 43%, even though millions in both countries endure great poverty. Even in China, which has traditionally had a healthier, non-dairy, vegetable-based diet, the number of overweight people jumped from 9% to 15% between the late 1980's and the early 1990's.
>
> Treating obesity-related illnesses costs Britain £2 billion a year, or 6% of the national health budget. The government has done little to curb the problem and indeed abandoned national targets to reduce obesity 10 years ago. Most experts believe the only solution is to encourage people to increase their exercise dramatically. It is no longer enough simply to walk instead of drive. Greater efforts need to be made to actually participate in sports.

Write the list.

PRACTICE 6

Situation: You work for Intervention Projects, Sandy Lane Estate, Barbados, West Indies. Mrs Marcia Lyttle, Managing Director, says to you that she is interested in an article she has read in *The Holders Hill Business Digest*, a local magazine. She asks you to **write a list** of the main points of the article. "In my next meeting with the Customer Service staff, we shall be talking about simple ways to impress existing and potential clients. This article is exactly the kind of thing that I am looking for."

> **TELEPHONE ETIQUETTE**
>
> Making a caller wait too long for someone to answer gives the impression that your business is not efficient. I always instruct my staff to try to answer the phone on the second ring. The third ring is acceptable, but any longer and, at best the caller may feel neglected. At worst, he or she may end the call and you will have annoyed a client.
>
> When people telephone your place of work, you certainly ought to thank them for calling, give them the name of your company so they know that they have reached the correct number, identify yourself and ask how you can assist them. For example an effective yet uncomplicated greeting is, "Thank you for calling the XYZ Institute. This is Barbara Taylor speaking. How may I help you?"
>
> The receptionist's role is vital to a firm's success. The receptionist presents the first impression most customers get of your business. Why not call your own number and see how you feel after listening to your receptionist or your automated message? Ask yourself the question, "Do I feel welcome? Does the first impression make me feel that the business is efficient?"
>
> A receptionist should speak slowly. Too often, I call a business and don't clearly hear the name of the business. I wonder if I have called the right place because the receptionist talked too quickly. I frequently get the impression that he or she is just dealing with the call as quickly as possible, rather than trying to help me, the caller.
>
> The telephone is a way of attracting and keeping customers, and if you follow some of this simple advice, your customers will get a more positive opinion of your business.

Write the list.

Situation: You are Customer Services Manager at Great Southern Railways, 30 - 32 Church Road, Treganna, St Ives, Cornwall, TR6 8BB. Tel: 01736 799 541 Fax: 01736 785 255.

You have just received the following letter.

Tel: 020 5569 3614

47 Holland Street
London
SE1 9KL

Customer Services Manager
Great Southern Railways
30 - 32 Church Road
Treganna
St Ives
Cornwall
TR6 8BB

13 September …

Dear Sir / Madam

I am a Sales Representative for Newton & Jupiter Ltd.

On 8 September I travelled by train to an important meeting in Bristol. Not only did the train leave an hour later than planned but it was delayed a further 45 minutes en route. No information was given as to why the train was delayed. The result was that I arrived almost two hours late for my appointment. Fortunately I had used my mobile to telephone ahead and advise my clients of the delay. Unfortunately my clients were unable to rearrange their schedule so the meeting had to be cancelled. Both they and I were extremely unhappy about this.

I would like a refund for my ticket and an explanation as to why the train was so delayed.

I look forward to hearing from you.

Yours faithfully
Janet Mills
Janet Mills (Mrs)

Your assistant has checked the details and left you the notes below. Reply to Mrs Mills apologising and explaining the reasons for the delay. Great Southern Railways do not usually refund money unless trains are cancelled. You decide, however, to exchange the ticket Mrs Mills used for a new ticket.

Complaint - Mrs Mills

Train left station 1 hour late because of bomb hoax

No information given to public to avoid panic

Further 45 minute delay caused by signal failure

Write the reply.

Situation: You work at Westbank Hotel and Conference Centre, 23 - 25 New Mount Street, Bath, Avon, BA1 8DF. Tel: 01225 456 666 Fax: 01225 456 600 E-mail: info@westbankhotel.co.uk Website: www.westbankhotel.co.uk The Manager is Mrs Esther Woodford.

Mrs Woodford gives you the following letter and asks you to draft a reply in her name.

Solpro Properties
44 Marylands Avenue
New Romney
Kent
TN28 8FR

Westbank Hotel and Conference Centre
23 - 25 New Mount Street
Bath
Avon
BA1 8DF

12 August …

Dear Sir/Madam

We are a building company specialising in building retirement flats for older people. We are organising our annual sales conference and have decided to approach you on recommendation from one of our suppliers.

We are planning to hold the sales conference from October 12 to 14 inclusive. It is normally attended by between 80 and 100 sales people so we will need a conference room which is large enough and which has good acoustics. Light refreshments throughout the day will also be required. Each of our delegates will need single accommodation and full board over the three days. Some of the participants are vegetarian and one member of the sales staff is in a wheelchair. Please let me know if you are able to fulfil our requirements.

Yours faithfully
Zoe Henry
Zoe Henry (Miss)

Mrs Woodford says, "I've checked the reservations calendar and there is no problem with accommodation for those dates. Can you check the availability for the conference rooms and reply to her? Don't forget to mention the new Relaxation Centre and tell her that we would need final figures by mid-September. Oh yes, we would also need to know if the vegetarians eat fish and eggs or not."

WEEK 41 **Availability**	**Mendip Conference Room**	**Stowe Conference Room**	**Cotswold Conference Room**	**Cheddar Conference Room**
Capacity	*90*	*140*	*110*	*40*
10 October	University – Conference	RTM Technics – Conference	Mr Tarre – Retirement Party	Free
11 October	T&G Sales Conference	RTM Technics – Conference	ST plc – AGM	A&M – AGM
12 October	Free	Free	Free	Free
13 October	Free	Greg Ltd – Training	Free	Tony Yair – 40th Birthday Party.
14 October	8pm Ladies Club Evening Meeting	Free	BC Petrol Training	In-house Staff Training
15 October	Mr Jackson - Wedding	Mr Hartfeld - Wedding	BC Petrol Training	Free

Draft the letter.

Situation: You work at Smith's Transport, a specialist haulage contractor. The address is Unit 350, Glenfield Industrial Estate, Bury, Lancashire, BL8 5DX. Tel: 0161 764 5896 Fax: 0161 765 5892. The Transport Manager is Mr Brian Ferguson.

Mr Ferguson has received the following enquiry from Coolit Ltd, a large frozen food processing company.

Coolit Ltd
22 Wardle Business Park, King's Street, Knutsford, Cheshire, WA16 6JD
Tel: 01565 98 32 65 Fax: 01565 98 3266

Mr Brian Ferguson
Transport Manager
Smith's Transport
Unit 350
Glenfield Industrial Estate
Bury
Lancashire
BL8 5DX

24 April …

Dear Mr Ferguson

Your company has been recommended to us by our local Chamber of Commerce.

We are a large frozen food processor and at present deliver all of our own produce. We are now starting to supply throughout the UK and are looking for a contractor who has the equipment and expertise to take over all of our deliveries.

Would you be interested in tendering for this contract?

Yours sincerely

J. Brown

John Brown (Mr)

Mr Ferguson leaves you the notes below and asks you to draft a reply ready for his signature.

Coolit Enquiry

Large fleet of 70+ refrigerated lorries

Daily deliveries to all parts of the UK

Storage facilities if needed

Suggest meeting to discuss details - either in their company or here

Draft the letter.

STAGE 6: CHECK YOUR WORK

CHECKLIST: LETTERS

1	Have you completed the task?	
2	Is the layout correct?	
3	Are the sender's details and the recipient's details correct?	
4	Is the date appropriate?	
5	Have you included all the relevant information?	
6	Have you ordered the information in the best way?	
7	Is the language appropriate for a letter?	
8	Have you checked spelling, grammar and punctuation?	

OPENING OF READING SHOP

24 – 26 High Street, Reading
Sat. 3 March

11am	*Speech by Sally Taylor, MP for Reading*
11.15	*Official Opening by Richard Hancock*
11.25	*Thanks by Roger Stanton, MD of Fulton's Bookshops*
11.30 - 12.30	*Buffet lunch*
13.00	*Book signing by two well-known authors*

Draft the letter.

STAGE 1: IDENTIFY THE TASK

Write the letter.

STAGE 2: LAYOUT

Sender's address:	Fulton's Bookshop, Ringway House, Kelvin Road, Enfield, Middlesex, EN3 4RT
Recipient's name:	Mr Richard Hancock
Recipient's address:	8 Mollison Avenue, Carmarthen, Dyfed, SA33 7EE
Appropriate date:	15 February …
Correct salutation:	Dear Mr Hancock
Correct complimentary close:	Yours sincerely
Sender's signature:	no signature
Sender's name:	Ruth Lea
Sender's position:	Manager

STAGE 3: IDENTIFY RELEVANT INFORMATION

- thanks for letter 12 Feb
- pleased Mr H accepted
- details of day's plan
- directions to get to shop
- address of new shop
- ask if Mr H needs collecting from station/ airport

STAGE 4: GROUP/ORDER RELEVANT INFORMATION

1 Thank you for letter of 12 February.
2 Pleased Mr H able to accept invitation.
3 Details of day's plan (from plan of opening).
4 Address of new shop in Reading.
5 Directions to get to shop by car (and where to park).
6 Ask if Mr H needs collecting from station.

STAGE 5: WRITE THE LETTER

Fulton's Bookshop
Ringway House, Kelvin Road, Enfield, Middlesex, EN3 4RT
Tel: 020 5631 8899 Fax: 020 5631 8870
Website: www.fultons.co.uk
Email: info@fultons.co.uk

Mr Richard Hancock
8 Mollison Avenue
Carmarthen
Dyfed
SA33 7EE

15 February …

Dear Mr Hancock

Thank you for your letter of 12 February. I am pleased that you are able to accept our invitation to open Fulton's new bookshop in Reading on Saturday 3 March.

The opening starts at 11 o'clock with a speech by Sally Taylor, the MP for Reading. The official opening of the shop is at 11.15 and this will be followed by a speech of thanks by Roger Stanton, the Managing Director of Fulton's Bookshops. From 11.30 to 12.30 there will be a buffet lunch followed by a book signing session by two well-known authors.

The address of the shop is 24 – 26 High Street, Reading. If you are coming by car follow signs for the town centre and then for Enton Car Park. We have 5 reserved spaces on the first floor, which are marked. Park your car here. Go out of the pedestrian entrance into High Street. Turn left and our new shop is 100 metres along High Street, on the right hand side of the road. If you are coming by train please let us know when you will arrive and we will collect you from the station.

Yours sincerely

Ruth Lea
Manager

STAGE 6: CHECK YOUR WORK

CHECKLIST: LETTERS

1	Have you completed the task?	✓
2	Is the layout correct?	✓
3	Are the sender's details and the recipient's details correct?	✓
4	Is the date appropriate?	✓
5	Have you included all the relevant information?	✓
6	Have you ordered the information in the best way?	✓
7	Is the language appropriate for a letter?	✓
8	Have you checked spelling, grammar and punctuation?	✓

YOUR EXAMPLE

Situation: You are Sales Assistant at ACE Worldwide Travel, 77 - 81 Bridge Street, Formby, Liverpool, L37 7WE. Tel: 01704 221 6594 Fax: 01704 221 9658.
The Manager is Miss Dorothy MacArthur.

Miss MacArthur asks you to reply to a letter from Greenwood Juniors Football Club.

Tel: 0113 896 321

Greenwood Juniors Football Club
C/o Mr Ian Pearson
24 Ashby Road
Manchester
M14 3HS

ACE Worldwide Travel
77 - 81 Bridge Street
Formby
Liverpool
L37 7WE

29 July ...

Dear Sirs

Between 1 and 21 September the Greenwood Juniors Football Club is taking part in an international schoolboys football tournament in Paris. There will be a total of 22 people in the party including 18 who are under 16 years of age. We would ideally like to depart from Manchester Airport on the morning of 1 September returning in the afternoon of 21 September. Could you please quote your cheapest prices? Can you also recommend a hotel, preferably one near to a park, so that we can use it for training?

If you need any more information please do not hesitate to contact me.

Yours faithfully

Ian Pearson

Ian Pearson

You check the flight details and see that there is only one flight from Manchester to Paris available, although there is a choice on the return flight. Write a letter to Mr Pearson explaining the flight details. Miss MacArthur says, "Don't forget to tell him that once the flight is booked, it can't be cancelled, so no refunds. We need 20% deposit payable when he confirms the booking and the remainder 14 days before travel. Suggest the website sporthotel.com for hotel details. If he hasn't got access to the internet then he can call into the shop and we can look it up with him."

Date	Flight	Dep. Time	Seats available	Price	Discounts for under 16's
September 1	Manchester - Paris	0545	19	£109	25%
September 1	Manchester - Paris	0615	22	£48	-
September 1	Manchester - Paris	1105	12	£59	-
September 21	Paris - Manchester	1335	25	£49	-
September 21	Paris - Manchester	1500	40	£128	40%
September 21	Paris - Manchester	1630	32	£99	30%

Draft the letter.

STAGE 1: IDENTIFY THE TASK

....

STAGE 2: LAYOUT

Sender's address: ....

Recipient's name: ....

Recipient's address: ....

Appropriate date: ....

Correct salutation: ....

Correct complimentary close: ....

Sender's signature: ....

Sender's name: ....

Sender's position: ....

STAGE 3: IDENTIFY RELEVANT INFORMATION

....

....

....

....

....

....

....

....

....

....

STAGE 4: GROUP/ORDER RELEVANT INFORMATION

....

....

....

....

....

....

....

....

....

....

PRACTICE 4

Situation: You work at GSL International Recruitment Agency, 17 Quai d'Orsay, 75007 Paris. Tel. 33/ 1 40 62 55 41 Fax 33/ 1 40 62 56 92. The Manager is Mr Alain Saille.

Mr Saille hands you the following letter and asks you to reply to it.

Auton Software
Unit 19, Business Square, Great Guildford Street, London SE1 0HS
Website: www.auton.com Tel: 020 9876 5544 Fax: 020 9876 5654

GSL International Recruitment Agency
17 Quai d'Orsay
F-75007 Paris
France

12 January ...

Dear Sirs

We recently wrote to you enquiring about your services. We have looked through your terms and conditions and found them to be satisfactory.

We are a small software company established 7 years ago specialising in accountancy programmes for small businesses. We are looking for a sales person responsible for developing sales in France. The person will work from home and a car will be provided. We need someone who speaks fluent French and English, has experience in accounting and is familiar with computers. It would be preferable if the person is familiar with the French taxation system. It would be an advantage if they had a background in sales. The salary is negotiable. We would require the successful candidate to start work on 1 May.

I look forward to hearing from you.

Yours faithfully
J. Wright
Jonathan Wright (Dr)
Managing Director

Mr Saille adds, "I've entered the details into the computer and printed out a list of possible candidates. See who would be best for the job and draft a letter ready for my signature. Send a copy of the CV with the letter and suggest an interview with the proposed candidate in our rooms here. If they want they can interview any other suitable candidates at the same time."

Name	**Fluent Languages**	**Degree**	**Previous Experience**	**Computer Skills**	**Driving Licence**
Natalie Morley	Ital, Fr, Eng	Economics	Accounts Clerk Stockbroker	V. good	No
Gisele Devreux	Eng, Fr	French Literature	Sales Rep Credit Controller	Good	Yes
Lorraine Barrymore	Fr, Eng	Accountancy	Accountant Tax Inspector	V. good	Yes
Christian Moreaux	Eng, Sp, Fr	No degree	Tax Clerk Sales Manager	Good	Yes
Michel Lamaison	Fr, Eng	Information Technology	Software Engineer Software Sales Rep	Excellent	Yes
Thierry Meyer	Germ, Eng, Fr	Business Studies	Software Sales Rep Financial Manager	Excellent	Yes

Draft the letter.

PRACTICE 5

Situation: You work at Global Office Supplies, PO Box 340, Borehamwood, Herts, WD6 1LT. Tel: 020 2369 5846 Fax: 020 2369 5700. The Sales Manager is Mr Max Humphreys.

Mr Humphreys gives you the following letter and asks you to write a reply ready for his signature.

Wiseman Medical Supplies
56 Eldon Road, Leith, Edinburgh EH1 3WP
Tel: 0131 225 8787 Fax: 0131 225 8687

Mr Max Humphreys
Sales Manager
Global Office Supplies
PO Box 340
Borehamwood
Herts
WD6 1LT

22 January …

Dear Mr Humphreys

We have been working with your company for 3 years and so far have been perfectly happy with the service we have received.

Recently, however, several mistakes have been made which give me cause for some concern.

On your invoice dated 10 January no discount was shown and your invoice dated 17 January listed 3 items which we had not ordered. Furthermore the delivery on 12 January contained some packing material which we did not request. The delivery which arrived yesterday did not contain the labels which we had requested urgently and there was no explanation as to where they were.

As we supply medical goods to hospitals it is of utmost importance that we have the correct packing materials and labels when we require them.

If your service does not improve immediately we will have to find an alternative supplier.

Yours sincerely
Pat Rhodes
Patrick Rhodes (Mr)
Director

You check the situation and make the following notes.

Missing labels sent by express courier - return other things at our costs
Many staff have been off work due to flu epidemic
Other staff working long hours / overtime to cover
Invoice errors
- *issued by a temporary member of staff (no longer with us)*
- *he didn't know Wiseman eligible for discount*
- *credit note will be issued*

Many apologies for all problems
First time it's happened – not prepared for epidemic
Staff nearly all back at work
Assure him it won't happen again

Write the reply.

PRACTICE 6

Situation: You work at Adonis Model Agency, Königsallee 15, 40210 Düsseldorf, Germany. Tel: 0211/ 37 64 27 Fax: 0211/ 37 64 0. The Agency Manager is Mrs Ursula Zimmermann.

Mrs Zimmermann says, "Look at this letter, this is great news. IT fashion magazine want to interview Gisele, the model we signed up last month, and may want to use her for the front cover. Check Gisele's diary and write a reply in my name. I want to be there as this is her first big interview."

IT Fashion Magazine
IT House, Edgware, London NW3 5YH
Tel: 020 3654 1212 Fax: 020 3654 9821 Website: www.itfashion.co.uk

Adonis Model Agency
Bookings Manager
Königsallee 15
D-40210 Düsseldorf
Germany

29 May …

Dear Sir / Madam

As you may be aware we have a regular interview spot in our international fashion magazine for new and upcoming models. The aim of this is to find out something about the model and discuss his or her interests.

In one of our forthcoming issues we would like to interview Gisele who we have been informed is contracted to your agency. We would like to interview her in an informal environment, perhaps in a hotel room or an apartment. If we are satisfied with the photographs we may wish to use her face on the front cover of the issue.

We would like the interview to be held in the week beginning Monday 12 June in Düsseldorf. Please let us know if you are in agreement with the interview and when / where would be convenient.

Yours faithfully
Jan Morgan
Jancis Morgan (Ms)
Editor

Mrs Zimmermann adds, "I can't change my meeting in the afternoon of the twelfth but I can manage any other day next week. Offer to collect them from the airport and ask them what kind of things they want to know about her." Look at the diary for Gisele and write the reply.

			Model: GISELE
	Morning	**Afternoon**	**Evening**
June 12 Monday	Photo session in-house		Modelling at Dolitti & Marcus fashion show
June 13 Tuesday	Hair & Beauty International Trade Fair	Meeting with JEUNE Cosmetics (contract?)	
June 14 Wednesday		Photo session – GIL's new fashion collection	Viewing Ralf Mannes fashion show
June 15 Thursday	Trial session with Jay Cooper, fashion designer		
June 16 Friday	11–15.30 NJR hair products demonstration on stand	Hans Braun meeting re HGH new mailorder catalogue	

Write the reply.

REVISION TEST

QUESTION	ANSWER ON PAGE
1	3
2	11
3	19
4	28
5	39
6	48
7	58

QUESTION 1

Situation: You work at RJS Cutting Machines, a company which manufactures and services fabric cutting machines.

You have just received a telephone call from Mr Lawdon, an important customer, who was very unhappy. Last week Mr Lawdon bought two machines from your company. Both the machines have broken down and you have agreed to go to his factory first thing in the morning to try and repair the machines. Write a memo to your assistant, Steve Hill, explaining why you will be out of the office tomorrow and asking him to carry out the duties listed below. Tell him you should be back in the office by mid-afternoon.

TO DO LIST

- *Phone Andrew (Engineering Dept.) - explain situation, say I might call for help.*
- *Phone Susan (Planning Dept) - ask for availability on new FXL 9000 cutting machine.*
- *Meeting at 10am - Karen Locke (Ingar Co.) - new customer*
  - show round factory, demonstrate FXL 9000.
- *FXL 7500 model - Find out if situation with faulty components been resolved?*
  If yes, find out delivery time? Valerie will know (Ext. 459).

Write the memo.

QUESTION 2

Situation: You work for VIP Pass, a company offering access to over 250 VIP airport lounges worldwide.

Your boss, Mr Richard Crosby asks you to write a leaflet for him, which can be handed out to passengers in airport departure lounges. He gives you the following information.

VIP Pass offers frequent travellers, especially business travellers, the opportunity to get away from busy airport terminals and to enjoy the peace and tranquillity offered by a VIP lounge. VIP lounges provide the business traveller with everything they are likely to need. Whether they need to phone the office or home, send that important fax or simply surf the internet, VIP Pass makes it possible. Or you can simply enjoy a complimentary light refreshment whilst reading the latest news in one of the many newspapers available free of charge. VIP Pass is so easy to use, where and whenever you find yourself waiting for a flight. For more info and to see for yourself how inexpensive it is visit us at www.vippass.com For your ease and convenience you can even join on-line.

Write the leaflet.

QUESTION 3

Situation: You work for Roberts Ltd, a manufacturer of sports clothing, based at Unit 78, Monument Industrial Park, Chalgrove, Oxford OX44 7YB. Tel: 01865 400 987 Fax: 01865 400 555.

The Shop Manager, Mrs Patricia Nelson, asks you to write a notice for her to display the times of factory tours. The notice will be put in the window of the factory shop.

Visit factory - Free entry - clothing from start to finish. Times: Jan - Dec. Mon - Thu 10.30, 11.30, 1.30, 2.30 (or by appointment) Fri (morning only) excl. public / local hols
Tour approx 40 mins. - Specially built factory.

Write the notice.

QUESTION 4

Situation: You work in the Customer Services Department of Grangetown Garages in Newcastle-upon-Tyne. The Managing Director is Mr Rob Sherwood.

Every time a customer has their car serviced you send a 'customer satisfaction questionnaire' out to them. Mr Sherwood instructs you to write a report on customer responses to the questionnaire to see if they are happy with the services carried out. He wants the report as soon as possible. You have analysed customers' replies for the last 3 months and have made the following notes.

Re Customer Satisfaction Questionnaire

105 cars serviced - 78 replies received (not all completed)

1 Are customers satisfied with service?
Yes (Y) 51% No (N) 39% Don't know (DK) 10%

Comments:
Mr B "don't notice any difference"
Mrs Y "car was fine before and is fine now"

2 Are customers satisfied with cost?
Y 23% N 65% DK 12%

Comments:
Mrs D "replacing parts - how do I know if they do?"
Mr G "all the costs are for labour"

3 Are customers satisfied with length of service?
Y 25% N 48% DK 27%

General
No problem for people working full-time - leave car in garage all day
Big problem for others, eg part-time workers/ single mothers/ young people
- We can't tell them how long service will last
- Have to wait in showroom (sometimes up to 4 hours!)

4 Are customers satisfied with work carried out?
Y 19% N 19% DK 62%

Comments
Mr B "I'm not a mechanic!"
Mrs R "how do I know?"

5 Other comments

Over half said showroom unfriendly
("not very light", "not very clean", "old cups lying around")

Other suggestions:
14 people suggested free coffee in showroom
21 suggested TV in showroom
9 suggested play area for kids

Write the report.

QUESTION 5

Situation: You work for CPI international airlines.

You company has recently installed a new self-service check-in system called 'Check & Go'. Your boss asks you to write an article for your airline's passenger magazine explaining the new system and encouraging people to use it. Here are your notes:

'Check & Go' – new time-saving idea
Check in automatically and get boarding card
- no queue
How it works: Put ticket into machine
Flight details are shown on screen
Check details are correct & press 'confirm' button
Answer usual questions about luggage, passport, etc
Available seats appear on screen, select seat & press 'confirm'
Boarding pass printed
Go straight to gate.
'C&G' computer terminals installed in all UK airports
Only for passengers with pre-paid ticket & hand-luggage

Write the article.

QUESTION 6

Situation: You work for Hearnsey Castle Gardens Ltd.

This evening you are going to give a talk to a group of visiting French tourists. Use the information below and make a list to use during your talk.

Hearnsey Castle Gardens are situated two and a half miles from the town centre on the B3258 road. The telephone number for the estate office is (01587) 720145 and for the restaurant is (01587) 741596. The gardens are open 7 days a week throughout the year. Bookings from organised groups are welcome. During the summer months, which is from end of March to end of October, the gardens are open from 11am – 5.30pm, and visitors can enjoy the Walled and Wild Gardens, Woodland Walks, Restaurant, other attractions and events. Season tickets are available during the summer season. In the winter months, from the end of October to March, visitors can enjoy the Walled and Wild Gardens and Woodland Walks during daylight hours. The large Domestic Garden is on a grand scale and lies at the centre of this traditional estate occupying a beautiful position on the River Severn. The garden is surrounded by magnificent hills and planted with a wide variety of mature specimen trees. Within the Walled Garden are greenhouses, which house many unusual species of plants, and an enchanting rose garden. The 12 acres of Wild Garden feature Woodland and Riverside Walks and provides a rich variety of colour and charm for both the keen gardener, or for the visitor simply wanting to enjoy a beautiful garden in peaceful surroundings. Other attractions include a Gift Shop, Children's Corner, Art Gallery and Tearoom/Restaurant. The Art Gallery is situated in the courtyard opposite the Restaurant and has regular exhibitions of invited artists throughout the summer. The Tearoom/Restaurant serves morning coffee, lunches and afternoon teas, 11am – 5.30pm. Bookings for lunch are advisable. Coach parties and evening parties can be admitted by arrangement. Special events are held throughout the summer. Information can be obtained from the estate office or from the local press. During the summer months the admission charge is £2 for adults and 50p for children (aged between 5 and 14). During the winter months the charge is £1 for adults and 50p for children (5 – 14). There is no charge for children under 5. Hearnsey is not a National Trust garden, but is privately owned and run by the Hearnsey family. We hope you will enjoy it with us.

Write the list.

QUESTION 7

Situation: You work at Fulton's Bookshop, Ringway House, Kelvin Road, Enfield, Middlesex, EN3 4RT. Tel: 020 5631 8899 Fax: 020 5631 8870 E-mail: info@fultons.co.uk Website: www.fultons.co.uk The Manager is Mrs Ruth Lea.

Mrs Lea has just received the following letter from Richard Hancock, a well-known sports personality. She hands it to you and asks you to draft a reply ready for her signature.

Tel: 01227 789 653

8 Mollison Avenue
Carmarthen
Dyfed
SA33 7EE

Mrs Ruth Lea
Fulton's Bookshop
Ringway House
Kelvin Road
Enfield
Middlesex
EN3 4RT

12 February ...

Dear Mrs Lea

Thank you for your kind invitation to open your new bookshop in Reading on Saturday 3 March. I would be most happy to do this.

Please could you send me some more details of the opening.

I am not sure yet whether I will be travelling by car or by train but if you could let me have directions as to how to get to the shop it would be much appreciated.

I look forward to hearing from you.

Yours sincerely
R. Hancock
Richard Hancock

Mrs Lea adds, "Here's the plan of the opening. Don't forget to include the address of the new shop and ask Mr Hancock to let me know if he needs collecting from the station."

OPENING OF READING SHOP

24 – 26 High Street, Reading
Sat. 3 March

11am	*Speech by Sally Taylor, MP for Reading*
11.15	*Official Opening by Richard Hancock*
11.25	*Thanks by Roger Stanton, MD of Fulton's Bookshops*
11.30 - 12.30	*Buffet lunch*
13.00	*Book signing by two well-known authors (still waiting for confirmation)*

Draft the letter.

FURTHER PRACTICE

QUESTION	TASK
1	LEAFLET
2	MEMO
3	REPORT
4	LIST
5	ARTICLE
6	NOTICE
7	LETTER
8	NOTICE
9	MEMO
10	ARTICLE
11	LIST
12	REPORT
13	LETTER
14	LEAFLET
15	NOTICE
16	REPORT
17	LEAFLET
18	MEMO
19	LIST
20	LETTER

QUESTION 1 (LEAFLET)

Situation: You are the Manager of Harthill House, a large country house in Wallingford, Oxfordshire, OX10 7BN. Tel: 01865 256 588. The house was built in the 11th century and now belongs to the National Trust. It is open to the public and regularly holds special events.

You decide to produce a leaflet informing the public about your mid-summer fair. You send the following email to your assistant Mike Ansell.

A Candidate

To: Mike Ansell
From: Stuart Sykes
Date: 1st May
Subject: Mid-Summer Fair

Would you write a leaflet which we can use to publicise the Mid-Summer Fair on Saturday and Sunday 21st and 22nd June? This year it will be open both days from 11am to 4pm. There will be a number of special offers including discounts on Harthill ales in the brewery shop.

There will be a sale of crafts and antiques in a tent on the front lawn and a variety of stalls in the gardens selling plants. There'll be the usual chance to ride a horse and there'll be a bouncy castle, which always proves popular with the kids. This year for the first time we have a company offering helicopter rides. The sheepdog display will take place as usual on Sunday at 3pm. The Cottage Restaurant will be open all day serving both lunches and afternoon teas.

We have engaged a well known local music band, Just Red, who will perform on Sunday at 1pm.

Make sure you mention that this will be a great chance to view the house and gardens and that it is free of charge. If there are any enquiries tell people to ring 01586 326 589.

Write the leaflet.

QUESTION 2 (MEMO)

Situation: You work at GENUS Biotechnology plc.

Recently a newspaper article reported details of a new product your company is developing to fight heart disease. Many of the details were correct and must have been supplied by an employee of the company. Your boss, Mrs Suzanne Hayes, is very angry and tells you to write a memo to all staff from her. She gives you the following notes.

Newspaper has DETAILED information about our product.
Very important info - could help competitors!!!.
CANNOT HAPPEN AGAIN.
Tell staff - all company information re developments is strictly confidential.
- don't discuss with anyone not from company
Be careful of unusual telephone calls. *Anything suspicious, contact me.*

Write the memo.

QUESTION 3 (REPORT)

Situation: You are a Research Assistant at IRS, an independent market research company.

Your company has been contacted by Dial-up Bank, which specialises in telephone banking. Three months ago Dial-up Bank introduced new guidelines for all its telephone operators following complaints from customers. Mrs Gaby Silver, Customer Services Manager of Dial-up Bank, has commissioned your company to write a report on whether these guidelines are being followed. Here are your notes.

Called 78 times. Period covered – fortnight. Tried to do various tasks (everyday & specific).

Operators' Guidelines	My Comments
Answer within 5 rings	*90% OK (longest wait - 8 rings)*
Always give your name to customers	*100% - but name not always clear - had to ask operator to repeat on several occasions*
Inform customer that call is recorded	*less than 50% - when I asked why, only one person knew (training & security)*
Carry out security check (ask for date of birth and postcode)	*100% always asked. I gave wrong information 5 times - operators pointed this out each time*
Carry out customer wishes	*Everyday tasks no problem eg transfers or ordering cheque books or checking balance Other tasks not so good - asked for exchange rates and was kept waiting for 8 minutes and then given wrong information - tried to do international transfer - passed on 3 times and then cut off.*
Transfer complaints to superior	*Most times (had to ask to speak to supervisor 2 out of 12 times)*
Other Comments	*- Often engaged & can't get through*

Write the report.

QUESTION 4 (LIST)

Situation: You work for Eyecare, a nationwide organisation of more than 500 opticians throughout the UK.

You are to give a talk to university students at a conference in London. Make a list of the main points to refer to during your talk from the article below.

Eyesight is too precious to take chances with. Everyone needs to be sure that they get excellent advice, care and treatment when they visit their opticians. But they also want to make sure that it isn't going to cost an arm and a leg too! That's why many opticians belong to Eyecare – a nationwide organisation of more than 500 opticians throughout the UK. At Eyecare customers not only get professional care, but friendly and personal service too. Eyecare opticians have also agreed to provide a national standard of professional care, which means customers benefit from the best of both worlds – friendly, local care with the back-up of a national organisation. Eyecare opticians are committed to providing their customers with regular comprehensive eye examinations as well as advice on general eye health and safety. They are also in a position to provide expert advice on the choice of spectacles or contact lenses. Information on children's requirements is available so parents are aware of their children's special needs. All Eyecare opticians only employ the best fully qualified staff. A one year's guarantee against faulty manufacture is also provided on all spectacles. It doesn't matter where you are in the UK there is an Eyecare optician near you. So when you see the red and blue Eyecare symbol you know that it's the sign for professional eye care. You can also be sure that you will get value for money.

Write the list.

QUESTION 5 (ARTICLE)

Situation: You work for Express Couriers Ltd.

Jenny Ross, Marketing Manager of Express Couriers Ltd, has asked you to write an article for the company's magazine Express News. Your company has recently introduced a new guaranteed next day delivery service "Special Delivery" which has already had great success. She gives you this list of the main points she wants you to include.

Special Delivery

1 "Special Delivery" (SD) set up end of last year.

2 SD takes over from "Next Day Plus" (ND+) service.

3 Recent survey rated SD best for cost, speed & reliability.

4 Guarantees next day delivery by 12 o'clock - UK wide.

5 Special packaging for customers free of charge.

6 Sales of "SD" to date - 24% up on former ND+ service.

7 Quotes from me:
- "easier/better service"
- "more effective and reliable than competitors"
- "many companies choosing it, makes good business sense."

Write the article.

QUESTION 6 (NOTICE)

Situation: You own and run RJS Photographic Studio.

You arrive at work to find a hole in the roof of the reception area and rainwater pouring in. When the roofing contractor arrives he says that he will need all day to repair the roof. Write a notice to be placed in the front window. Explain the situation and apologise to customers. Inform them to use the side entrance in South Street.

Write the notice.

QUESTION 7 (LETTER)

Situation: You work at PLT Cinema, 9 King's Road, Exeter, EX5 4HG. Tel: 01392 426 255.
The Managing Director is Mr Hugh Phillips.

Mr Phillips gives you the following letter and says, "Can you remember James Thomson who used to work here? Well, it sounds as though he's doing very well. Here's a request for a reference for him from MCME."

M.C.M.E
Medway Cinema Multiplex Entertainment
Chatham, Kent, TN14 7TG
Tel: 01392 426 255

PLT Cinema
Mr Hugh Phillips
Managing Director
9 King's Road
Exeter
EX5 4HG

23 March …

Dear Mr Phillips

Reference – James Thomson

We have received an application for the job of Manager in one of our multiplex cinemas from James Thomson, a former employee of yours. He has given us your name as a referee. The position of Manager for which he has applied would require him to deal with the public on a regular face-to-face basis. He would be responsible for resolving any problems immediately and for ensuring the smooth running of the multiplex site.

Please can you supply us with a reference.

Yours sincerely
M. George
Michelle George (Miss)
Managing Director

Mr Phillips adds, "Use the information from his personnel file and add that he was an excellent employee, an asset to the company and that I have no hesitation in recommending him for the job. Draft the letter ready for my signature and tell her to contact me if she wants any more information."

PERSONNEL FILE **PRIVATE AND CONFIDENTIAL**

Name:	James Thomson
Employed from:	14 June 1994
Employed to:	21 December 1999
Positions held:	Assistant Cinematographer Chief Cinematographer Assistant Manager
Reason for leaving:	Wanted more contact with people Got new job with the IR Theatre and Filmhouse as Promotional Manager
General comments:	Always well-dressed, punctual, reliable Excellent people skills, good communicator Well-liked and respected by staff and management.

Draft the letter.

QUESTION 8 (NOTICE)

Setting: You and your wife have recently taken over the Mayflower Restaurant, 6 Highgate, Taunton, TN7 6PW, Somerset. Tel: 01596 986 555.You decide to write a notice to hang up in your shop window announcing the re-opening of the restaurant. Use the following notes.

- All-day snacks, lunches and coffee (10 - 4 Mon - Sun).
- Restaurant open (evening meals) Thurs - Sat 7 - 9. Must book.
- November - Special offer / dinner menu 15% discount (incl. drinks & wine).

Write the notice.

QUESTION 9 (MEMO)

Situation: You are the MD of WAKO Semi Conductors.

Your company has just received confirmation of a big export order to Japan. Write a memo to all staff informing them of this and telling them that you are going to offer Japanese courses. Don't forget to thank them for their help during the 3-day visit. Use the notes below and add anything else you think necessary.

Recent 3-day visit of Japanese delegation
- order now confirmed.

Only problem - lack of Japanese speakers in the company.

Planning to change this for future visits

- company will offer free language courses for all employees (Japanese).

Courses to start asap.

Write the memo.

QUESTION 10 (ARTICLE)

Setting: Mrs Claudia Hofer, the Human Resources Manager at Generali Stores, Graz, Austria says, "One of our local colleges has asked if a member of our staff will submit a short article for the college students' magazine about what it is like to work in a large department store."

Mrs Hofer asks you to **write the article**. She points out that it should be lively and likely to stimulate interest in the work. She suggests some of the points that you may wish to write about: meeting different people, discussing what they need, offering advice on different products and the prices, keeping up to date with new products, and how it can be a worthwhile and satisfying career. She says, "You may add anything else which you think relevant. You can, of course, leave out any of my suggestions."

The college wants the article to be about 4 or 5 paragraphs long.

Write the article.

QUESTION 11 (LIST)

Situation: The Head of the Finance Department says, "I have been asked to talk to trainee finance officers who are studying at a local college. The subject is 'Dealing With Debt'. Can you **write a list** of the main points from this article for me, please? It is exactly the kind of information that I will find useful." Here is the article:

How a small business can deal with late payment

Small companies have for years been at risk from slow payments by large clients. Serious late payment can even lead to bankruptcy in the worst cases. However, even if the amount owed is small, chasing payment is an everyday task for many small businesses.

To deal with the problem of late payments, there are several things you can consider:
You can print your terms and conditions for payment clearly on contracts. These terms should state the payment period for any invoice - quite often you would expect payment within 30 days, but this could be shorter or longer depending on your type of business. If you do this, no firm can easily use the excuse, "Oh, we are sorry. We did not know when you would expect us to pay."

You can offer a discount for early payment. For example, you can charge £500 + VAT for a service (or product), if the amount is settled within your stated payment period of 28 days, and £475 + VAT, if payment is made within 10 days. This is likely to encourage many clients to pay early. You will of course make less money on each deal, but that is surely better than having a client owing you the whole amount.

If a client has not paid on time, it is essential to pursue the debt. Always try to find a person to contact in the Accounts Department. A person who you have found to be helpful in the past is best, but any named person is better than just the "Accounts Department".

Politely ask for the payment to be made and, if the problem continues, you can consider charging interest on the overdue amount, or in the worst case, threaten the late payer with legal action. In these instances, you will probably not have any more business from that client, but do you really need clients who do not pay?

Write the list.

QUESTION 12 (REPORT)

Situation: 10 days ago SPT Group held a party to thank all employees for their help and support during the recent move of the company from its 150-year-old inner-city premises to a purpose-built factory in an out-of-town location. The party, which was organised by a local catering firm, was a complete disaster. Mr Ken Adams, MD, tells you to produce a report for the next manager's meeting as to what went wrong. You spend 3 days speaking to over 50 employees to find out their opinions and note down the main complaints.

Food looked like it had been prepared days before.
Little variety, not much of it.
Not enough waiting staff, untrained, unhelpful, untidy.
No soft drinks, no tea, only coffee and this was cold!
Plastic knives and forks, cardboard cups and plates.
Tablecloths dirty, no serviettes.

You also speak to Mrs Isobel Green, responsible for arranging the catering firm. She informs you that the firm was chosen simply on price as the company had a fixed budget and other firms were much more expensive. She says the firm was recommended to her.

Write the report.

QUESTION 13 (LETTER)

Situation: You are Sales Assistant at Caver House Stationers, 48 Halten Road, Plymouth, PL6 2XC. Tel: 01752 506 399 Fax: 01752 500 453. The Sales Manager is Mr Peter Richardson.

Mr Richardson gives you the following letter. He asks you to check the stock records and reply to it.

Burgess and Cope Solicitors
Callington Way, Tavistock, TK14 3NJ
Tel: 01752 639 544 Fax: 01752 639 555

Caver House Stationers
Mr Peter Richardson
Sales Manager
48 Halten Road
Plymouth
PL6 2XC

25 July …

Dear Mr Richardson

Mr Burgess has requested me to place an order for the following goods:

Qty	Description	Colour	Code	Unit price	Total
1 pack	STICKIT glue sticks (25 x 10g)		STK033	£23.50	£23.50
1 pack	LITE box files	yellow	LIT011	£50.50	£50.50
10 sets	A-Z board dividers		DIV101	£1.10	£11.00
2 boxes	C4 envelopes (self-seal, window)	white	ENV112	£8.50	£16.00
10 rolls	Low-noise packaging tape	clear	TPS233	£2.00	£20.00
2 packs	HB pencils		PNC1766	£6.25	£12.50
1 pack	Large lipped paper clips		PAC556	£1.75	£1.75
2 packs	YELO post-it notes		YEL991	£5.50	£11.00

Please can you confirm prices and let me know when you can deliver?

Yours sincerely

Janet Lawson

Janet Lawson (Miss)

You have checked the stock records and your current price list and made the notes below. Some of the prices quoted in the letter are from your last year's price list.

Qty	Description	Code	Price	*Notes*
1 pack	STICKIT glue sticks (25 x 10g)	STK033	£23.50	*OK - sent*
1 pack	LITE box files	LIT011	£50.50	*Current price £55.00 - check*
10 sets	A-Z board dividers	DIV101	£1.10	*Only 9 in stock - sent. 1 to follow*
2 boxes	C4 envelopes (self-seal, window)	ENV112	£8.50	*wrong total*
10 rolls	Low-noise packaging tape clear	TPS233	£2.00	*Not available. Send normal £1.50?*
2 packs	HB pencils	PNC1766	£6.25	*OK - sent*
1 pack	Large lipped paper clips	PAC556	£1.75	*OK - sent*
2 packs	YELO post-it notes	YEL991	£5.50	*Current price £5.75 - check*

Draft the letter.

QUESTION 14 (LEAFLET)

Setting: You work for Scotia Ferries, Unit 7, Limestone Road Technology Park, Belfast, Co. Antrim, BT15 3AN. Tel 01232 632 144. The company operates ferry services between Scotland and Northern Ireland. Mr Saville, the Marketing Manager, is based at the company's Stranraer offices in Scotland. You return from lunch to find the following telephone message left on your desk by one of your colleagues.

TELEPHONE MESSAGE

Time 13.20
Caller Mr Saville

Mr S. wants a leaflet about our new ferry for passengers. Wants you to include the following points:
• New fast ferry - largest in world. 2x faster than normal ferry (40 knots). Lots of space and very comfortable. Size of a football pitch - 120m x 40m. Can carry 1200 passengers.
• On-board entertainment includes live bands, kids entertainers, 'theme' cruises.
• On board facilities -: 3 lounges, restaurant, cinema, bar and kids play area.
• Quick check-in.
• Stranraer to Belfast = 99 mins.
He also said to mention that the facilities are all on one deck and to add whatever else you think may be important.

Jo

Write the leaflet.

QUESTION 15 (NOTICE)

Situation: You work at Dianella Superstore in Napier Road, Perth, Western Australia. At a recent Administration and Finance Meeting the following was part of the discussion:

Personnel Officer	*I'm a little worried that some staff are not helping us to keep our records accurate … if they change their home telephone number … well, I am just not being told … sometimes even changes of address, name … I am not informed.*
Head of Accounts	*Yes. It's a problem that I often come across … we sometimes find we try to pay an employee's wages into a bank account that no longer exists … They have changed banks … without telling us.*
Personnel Officer	*Many are not signing in and out properly … when they arrive at work and when they leave. I suppose if we didn't pay them when they …*
Head of Administration	*I agree that something has to be done … but not paying staff is much too harsh … I think we need to **write a notice** to remind staff …*
Personnel Officer	*We can put it in the staff rest-room. It will need to be a tactful reminder. Can we include in the notice the rules about our discounts to staff?*
Head of Administration	*Yes. The rules are quite simple … 20% off everything we sell … but … only 15% until they have worked here for a year …*
Personnel Officer	*That's right … and all items have to be paid for … They must not take anything home until all the money is paid.*
Head of Accounts	*We can deal with lost property in the same notice … shouldn't we ask people to give all lost property to the Security Officer? If not claimed … after 6 months …person who found it …*
Personnel Officer	*… can ask to keep it … The only thing that I ever found was a packet of sandwiches … I wonder what they were like after 6 months!*

Write the notice.

QUESTION 16 (REPORT)

Situation: You are European Sales Representative at ProActive plc, a manufacturer of sports equipment. Mr Graham Roslin, the Sales Manager, is your boss.

Last week you and a team of 3 sales staff were at the WRF International Fitness Exhibition in Berlin. Your boss asks you to write a report to justify the costs involved. Use the notes you made while you were at the exhibition to write the report.

> ***WRF Int. Fitness Ex.*** *22 - 26 Feb, Berlin* *Held every year, this year 10th year.*
> *176 exhibitors from 27 countries.*
> *Expected over 97,000 visitors (no final figures yet - but very busy every day). First two days trade only - many useful contacts, from sports clubs, private gyms, hotel, schools.*
> *Two contacts interested in distributing our models in Germany –*
> *Contact 1 owns chain of shops selling sports equipment*
> *Contact 2 owns warehouse & imports sports equipment for wholesale (is setting up website for direct sales).*
> *Trade visitors - most interest on stand in multigym equipment (particularly X5 model - perceived as very good value). 71 orders for X5. Public liked X4 home gym (important that it folds away), but wanted to buy from local distributor (potential distributor contacts in Germany above). Many other contacts from eastern European countries (distribution, but looking for long credit!). Value of orders was just below costs (hopefully repeat orders though). Also many useful contacts made and presence on international market platform very important.*

Write the report.

QUESTION 17 (LEAFLET)

Setting: You work for Sims Travel Co., who specialise in quality holiday villas in Spain, Portugal and France. Their address is Abbey House, 87 St. John's Street, Luton, Bedfordshire, LU3 1BB. Tel: 01582 779545 Freephone 0990 567 888. Mrs Heale, your boss, asks you to draft a leaflet to be sent out with a mailshot next month. Here are her notes.

> *Great choice: cosy cottages / splendid villas / renovated farmhouses. Beautiful locations: coast, countryside. All self-catering. Special offers for next year: 20% off a second holiday taken in same year / 4 weeks for price of 3 (low season only). Don't forget – our travel insurance (very competitive - £50 for year). More info - call freephone number.*

Write the leaflet.

QUESTION 18 (MEMO)

Situation: You are a secretary at Westhampton College, a private further education institute. The Principal of the college, Mrs Kirsty Doyle, is retiring at the end of next month after 27 years. Sara Richardson, Deputy Principal, asks you to write a memo to all Faculty Heads in her name. She gives you the following notes:

> *Mrs D's retirement - 19 August 14.30 / Sinclair Room (Engineering Faculty) / Formal dress.*
> *If not possible to go - inform me.*
> *Retirement card in my office - make sure everyone signs it.*

Write the memo.

QUESTION 19 (LIST)

Situation: You are going for an interview at Gilberts Co, a producer of port.

You want to make a good impression during the interview and are researching the company. You have downloaded some information from their website and to help you remember it you make a list of the major points.

A family story of port

Gilbert's was founded in Vila Nova de Gaia, at the mouth of the River Douro opposite Oporto, in 1815 by Alistair Gilbert, a member of a famous Scottish family.

The crest of the Gilbert's family shows an eagle and 3 feathers. The symbol of the eagle above the 3 feathers has become a symbol of the company and appears on the labels of every bottle of port produced by them.

In 1830 Alistair Gilbert instructed his son, Robert, to open an office in London, as almost all of the port was exported to Britain. Additional partners, mainly from two other families, brought further expertise into the company. The Fitzpatrick family joined the company in 1854 and managed the Portuguese end of the company. The McNeill family joined 7 years later. Even today, four generations on, there is still a member of the Fitzpatrick family on the board of Gilbert's Portugal.

Gilbert's value the close relationship which they have developed with the farmers who provide grapes and wine for the Gilbert's different blends of port. Many of these relationships go back over several generations. Unusually nowadays, there are no written contracts; a handshake is enough to seal an agreement.

Gilbert's has managed to maintain the feel of a family business right into the 20th century, and has managed at the same time to absorb many influences from Portugal. Since 1975 the Managing Director of Gilbert's Portugal has been Portuguese.

Since its beginnings in 1815 the company has expanded to become one of the largest port companies in the world.

Write the list.

QUESTION 20 (LETTER)

Setting: You are Marketing Assistant at Saracen Print Group, 17 Hammond Way, Swadlincote, Derby, DY12 6JH. Tel: 01283 550 223 Fax: 01283 550 294 Website: www.saracenprint.co.uk
The Sales Manager is Ms Pam Lichfield.

Ms Lichfield gives you the following letter from the Agency Manager at your local Regional Development Agency. She asks you to draft a reply ready for her signature.

DERDA
Derbyshire Regional Development Agency
25 Burton Road, Derby, DY6 6TG
Tel: 01283 995 648 Fax: 01283 956 321 Website: www.derda.co.uk

Saracen Print Group
17 Hammond Way
Swadlincote
Derby
DY12 6JH

5 September …

Dear Sirs

We are a new Regional Development Agency established by the government and are responsible for setting and implementing the agenda for long-term economic growth in our region. We are looking for a partner to provide all our agency's printwork and are writing to you to see if you would be interested in tendering for this contract.

I look forward to hearing from you.

Yours faithfully
C J Brendan
Craig Brendan
Agency Manager

Ms Lichfield adds, "This could be an important contract so mention these points I've noted down. Don't forget to say that the company was started in 1966 and now has over 100 employees."

Re: DERDA letter

Got new premises last year
- *purpose-built*
- *lots of parking space*
- *state-of-the-art 5-colour press*

All usual printing jobs undertaken / All work high quality / Good rates
We guarantee date of delivery

PLUS
- *In-house designer produces work in ready-to-print form (avoids technical problems & saves costs for customers)*
- *Specialist full-colour printing*
- *Full-colour digital printing (ideal for personalised work)*

Visit to factory?

Draft the letter.

ANSWERS

SECTIONS 1 – 7

YOUR EXAMPLE

SECTION 1:MEMOS

STAGE 1: IDENTIFY THE TASK
Write the memo.

STAGE 2: LAYOUT

To:	All staff
From:	Michael Rosselini
Subject:	Aaron Jackson's visit
Date:	Today's date

STAGE 3: IDENTIFY RELEVANT INFORMATION
- Aaron Jackson CEO visiting
- next Tuesday
- visit from 11 – 3
- interested in new gold strike
- mainly meetings with management
- may visit mine
- may talk to staff
- first visit
- important to make good impression

STAGE 4: GROUP/ORDER RELEVANT INFORMATION
1 Aaron Jackson CEO will visit next Tuesday from 11am - 3pm.
2 First visit so important to make good impression.
3 Main reason is new gold strike.
4 Mainly management meetings but may visit mine / speak to staff.

STAGE 5: WRITE THE MEMO

MEMO

To: All staff
From: Michael Rosselini
Subject: Aaron Jackson's visit
Date: Today's date

We have just had news that Aaron Jackson our Chief Executive Officer will visit the mine next Tuesday from 11am to 3pm. This will be his first visit to the mine and it is important that we make a good impression.

The main reason for his visit is that he is interested in the gold strike we made 2 days ago. He will mainly be involved in meetings with management but may wish to visit the mine and may want to speak to staff.

STAGE 6: CHECK YOUR WORK
CHECKLIST: MEMOS

1	Have you completed the task?	✓
2	Is the layout correct?	✓
3	Are the details correct (To: From: Date)?	✓
4	Does the subject line tell you briefly what the memo is about?	✓
5	Have you included all the relevant information?	✓
6	Have you ordered the information in the best way?	✓
7	Is the language appropriate for a memo?	✓
8	Have you checked spelling, grammar and punctuation?	✓

PRACTICE 1

MEMO

To: All staff
From: Your name
Subject: Redecorating of customer reception area
Date: Today's date

I have just been informed by the contractors redecorating the customer service area that they will now not be finished by Sunday night but will need all Monday as well. This will mean that on Monday we will be unable to re-open the customer service area and as a result customers will have to enter through the workshop.

Because of this would you please ensure that:

1 All passageways are kept clear.

2 All areas are kept clear of oil.

3 Great care is taken when reversing cars out of the garage.

4 Music is not so loud.

I would also ask staff to be friendly and helpful to customers at all times.

Y.N.

PRACTICE 2

MEMO

To: All staff
From: Mrs Hasten, Personnel Manager
Date: Today's date

Christmas Holiday Leave

As it is now December it is time that all employees arranged their Christmas holiday leave. If you haven't already done so contact Simon in Administration (Room 245 Ext. 450) with the dates you would like, as soon as possible.

I would like to remind all staff that if anyone has any holiday leave outstanding it must be taken before the end of the year and that it can't be paid out as salary.

Please note that December 25th and 26th are public holidays and are therefore in addition to your annual leave.

PRACTICE 3

SECTION 1:MEMOS

MEMO

To: All staff
From: Robert Principal, Chairman
Subject: Atlantic Pharmaceuticals in receivership
Date: Today's date

As you know the past months have been very difficult for us. We have lost many important customers because of the continuing strength of the pound which has made it very difficult for us to sell our pharmaceuticals abroad. At the same time our domestic sales have been badly affected by our UK customers taking advantage of the strong pound and buying their pharmaceuticals abroad.

Yesterday the bank stopped the extended credit facility for our company as a result of which we are no longer able to continue to operate and the company has been put into receivership. The receivers will take over the running of the company until a buyer is found.

We are optimistic that a buyer will soon be found to take over the company and that no jobs will be lost. In the meantime I would ask you carry on as normal. As soon as more information is available we will let you know.

PRACTICE 4

MEMO

To: All retail staff
From: Your name, Customer Services Manager
Date: Today's date

Company policy on exchanging goods

Many customers have complained recently about difficulties they have experienced when returning shoes they were not happy with. To avoid any further confusion please make sure that you read the following carefully.

When purchasing shoes customers should always be informed to keep their receipts and to return shoes within ten days if they are not satisfied.

When customers return goods:

1 Ask for their receipt.
2 Check the date on the receipt is not more that ten days ago.
3 Check the receipt is for the shoes they are returning.
4 Check the condition of the shoes and that they haven't been worn.
5 Check if the shoes are still in the original box.

If all of the above are OK offer to exchange the goods or if preferred grant a refund.

When exchanging shoes, they do not have to be the same price or even the same type. However, please note refunds are not available for shoes bought in the sale. Shoes bought in the sale can only be exchanged for other shoes in the sale of the same value.

PRACTICE 5

MEMO

To Team Leaders and Heads of Department
From A. Candidate
Date *Today's date*

Organising Meetings

Mr Miah has asked me to remind you of some important ways in which we can make certain that our meetings are effective.

AGENDA
- The agenda should be sent to participants before the day of the meeting so that people can think about the topics.
- The agenda must always be unambiguous and concise.

CHAIRPERSON
The main duty of a chairperson is to make certain that the meeting is efficiently run;
- Start and finish on time. Waiting for latecomers can only encourage people to be late.
- Keep strictly to the agenda. Do not allow deviation.
- Encourage everyone to participate but keep all discussion relevant.

OUTCOME
A successful meeting is often one that is brief and in which a decision is arrived at following everyone's participation.

PRACTICE 6

MEMO

To All Staff at Head Office
From A. Candidate
Subject Visit by new Public Relations Officer, Miss Maureen Flaherty
Date *Today's Date*

Miss Maureen Flaherty has recently been appointed as Public Relations Officer at Peerless Commodities. Although she does not officially start work here for a further six weeks, Miss Flaherty intends to visit us on Tuesday next week starting at 10 a.m.

The purpose of her visit is to:

- meet as many colleagues as possible
- learn more exactly what Peerless Commodities does
- form ideas for future publicity.

I shall be her guide for the day and introduce her to you. The visit is informal and the main idea is for her to meet as many of us as possible, to chat and for you to tell her any ideas that you have that may be useful to her.

A.C.

YOUR EXAMPLE

SECTION 2: LEAFLETS

STAGE 1: IDENTIFY THE TASK

Write the leaflet.

STAGE 2: LAYOUT

There are no special rules for layout, however, it must be easy to read, eye-catching and contain contact details and a date.

STAGE 3: IDENTIFY RELEVANT INFORMATION

- Elliot's Art & Framing
- address
- tel. no.
- large selection of frames
- contemporary and traditional
- frames made on site
- experience in framing oil paintings etc.
- certificate frames
- ready-made frames
- extensive range of materials
- materials for children
- gift vouchers
- exhibitions
- paintings, drawings, photographs for sale
- welcome to browse

STAGE 4: GROUP/ORDER RELEVANT INFORMATION

1 Elliot's Art & Framing.
2 Large selection of frames.
3 Contemporary and traditional.
4 Experience in framing oil paintings etc.
5 Certificate frames.
6 Ready-made frames.
7 Exhibitions.
8 Paintings, drawings, photographs for sale.
9 Welcome to browse.
10 Extensive range of materials.
11 Materials for children.
12 Gift vouchers.
13 Frames made on site.
14 Address & tel. no.
15 Date.

STAGE 5: WRITE THE LEAFLET

ELLIOT'S ART & FRAMING

We stock a wide selection of
CONTEMPORARY AND TRADITIONAL FRAMES
to suit your needs.

We have wide experience in framing all types of artwork including:

- oil paintings
- watercolours
- drawings
- photographs
- certificates

We have a large range of READY-MADE FRAMES for photographs and smaller pictures.

We hold
EXHIBITIONS
where
original paintings, drawings and photographs can be bought.

COME IN AND BROWSE - There is no obligation to buy!

We stock an extensive range of ARTISTS' MATERIALS:
oil paints
watercolour paints
paintbrushes and pencils
sketch boards
individual sheets of paper and card

We also have materials SUITABLE FOR CHILDREN:

fabric paints
face paints
paper and card in many different colours

GIFT VOUCHERS available from the value of £5 upwards.

All framing is carried out on site in our own workshop.

17 Ashby Road, Headington, Oxford OX2 9BN
Tel: 01865 288 944

Issued on (today's date)

STAGE 6: CHECK YOUR WORK

CHECKLIST: LEAFLETS

1	Have you completed the task?	✓
2	Is the layout correct?	✓
3	Have you included contact details?	✓
4	Have you included a date of issue?	✓
5	Have you included all the relevant information?	✓
6	Have you ordered the information in the best way?	✓
7	Is the language appropriate for a leaflet?	✓
8	Have you checked spelling, grammar and punctuation?	✓

PRACTICE 1

SECTION 2: LEAFLETS

HARVEY ALLEN FINE CASHMERE

Mill shop located at 74 New Leeds Road, Bradford, BD14 7AM
(5 miles north of Bradford on A650)

FREE PARKING

Experience the LUXURY of cashmere at COMPETITIVE PRICES direct from our own mill.

Ladies & gents cashmere & lambs wool knitwear in a variety of colours.

All major credit cards accepted.

TAX-FREE SHOPPING service available for non-EC visitors.

Open all year: Mon-Fri 0900 – 1700

Issued on (today's date)

PRACTICE 2

THE EXPERIENCE OF A LIFETIME
at
UNDER THE SEA'S AQUARIUM ENTERTAINMENT CENTRE

✷ Lots of fun for all the family ✷

Come face to face with Europe's largest collection of TIGER SHARKS.
Watch our divers HAND FEED THE FISH in this underwater world.
Speak to the divers using our state of the art communications system.
Walk through the UNDERWATER GLASS TUNNEL - the longest in the world.

More than 200 different species of fish and other creatures
CRABS and STARFISH

Large collection of PIRANHAS

Visit the REPTILE CENTRE and see the snakes and crocodiles.

Free FACE PAINTING for everyone

Take a souvenir home with you from our GIFT SHOP.

Don't forget to visit OUR UNDER THE SEA RESTAURANT to complete your day out.

Open 12 months of the year 0930 – 1800 (apart from public holidays)
Half price for children under the age of 16
Discounts for groups of more than 10 people

For an educational and interesting day out for the whole family contact:
Under the Sea Aquariums Ltd, Blackpool, Lancashire, FY11 8JH,Tel: 01253 564 888.

Details of special events and on-line booking through our Website: www.underthesea.co.uk
Issued on (today's date)

PRACTICE 3

SPECIAL OFFER
on all
SHORT BREAKS between January 1st and February 28th

3 NIGHTS BED AND BREAKFAST FOR THE PRICE OF 2

Normal price £72 pppn*
Special price £48 pppn*
SAVING = £24

All rooms en suite

Awarded 4-stars by Tourist Board

Restaurant open every evening with an extensive menu and large selection of fine wines.

For more information please contact:
Monkerston Country House Hotel
Adderston Road, Monkerston
Derbyshire, NH16 5TR.
Tel: 01659 7895 9685. Fax: 01659 7894 5612.
E-mail: info@monkerstonhouse.co.uk
Website: www.monkerstonhouse.co.uk

offer subject to availability
*per person per night
Issued on (today's date)

PRACTICE 4

THE BALLOON FLIGHT OF A LIFETIME
with
EAGLE FLIGHTS

Flights NATIONWIDE from a variety of locations
Book through your nearest office
CERTIFICATES for all first time balloonists
Corporate or private customers catered for
Unique photographic opportunity
DAILY FLIGHTS*
All pilots are fully qualified.
All equipment is state of the art.

SPECIAL OFFER JANUARY TO MARCH
FREE PHOTO at take-off

GIFT VOUCHERS available

Freephone: 0990 554 696
www.eagleflights.com
*weather permitting

Issued on (today's date)

PRACTICE 5

SECTION 2: LEAFLETS

SPECIAL NEW YEAR OFFER

Unbeatable internet only SALE NOW ON

175,000 seats
(Jan - Mar)

LONDON	**LONDON**	**LONDON**	**LONDON**	**LONDON**
to	to	to	to	to
BELFAST	**EDINBURGH**	**AMSTERDAM**	**ZURICH**	**ATHENS**
£25 return	**£30** return	**£40** return	**£50** return	**£70** return

Buy online www.flygo.com

BOOK NOW!
Offer must end midnight Tuesday 24 November.
EXCLUSIVELY AVAILABLE at www.flygo.com

Offer for travel between 10 January and 26 March only.
A Saturday night must be included.
Offer available on selected flights only subject to availability.
All fares exclude airport tax.
Issued on (today's date)

PRACTICE 6

ARE YOU GETTING THE BEST FROM YOUR INSURANCE COMPANY?

If you are over 50 Burrell Insurance can offer you better deals on:

HOME INSURANCE
Significant discounts for the over 50's
Free 24 hour Legal and Home Emergency Helplines

MOTOR INSURANCE
Up to 30% extra discount for over 50's
Additional discounts for low mileage drivers
RAC breakdown cover at special rates

PET INSURANCE
Covers vets' fees up to £500
Up to £300 if you lose your pet through theft or in an accident
Third party liability up to £1 million

TRAVEL INSURANCE
No maximum age limit
Medical expenses up to £2 million

CALL TODAY FOR YOUR FREE NO OBLIGATION QUOTATION
Freephone 0800 0107 0905
Issued on (today's date)

YOUR EXAMPLE

SECTION 3: NOTICES

STAGE 1: IDENTIFY THE TASK
Write the notice.

STAGE 2: LAYOUT
A notice requires a clear heading at the top. It must have the name and position of the person who wrote it at the bottom. It must have a date at the bottom.

STAGE 3: IDENTIFY RELEVANT INFORMATION

- Finchley Branch of National Bank
- 334 High Road, Finchley, London, N12 8PL
- Tel: 020 4655 6233
- Mrs Edith Knowles, Branch Manager
- closing Tue 25 Jun
- apologise/ inconvenience
- improve efficiency
- customers to Branch in Hardy Street
- directions/ location
- new tel no.

STAGE 4: GROUP/ORDER RELEVANT INFORMATION

1. Branch closed from Tuesday 25th June.
2. Use the National Bank at 45 Hardy Street.
3. 200 yards opposite main railway station.
4. New tel no: 020 4187 9853.
5. Rationalisation measures.
6. Regret inconvenience.
7. Mrs Edith Knowles, Branch Manager.
8. National Bank Finchley Branch.
9. 334 High Road, Finchley, London, N12 8PL.
10. Tel: 020 4655 6233.

STAGE 5: WRITE THE NOTICE

ALL CUSTOMERS

Please note this Branch will be closed from Tuesday 25th June.

Would all customers please use the National Bank's Branch at
45 Hardy Street
The branch is 200 metres from here, opposite the main railway station.
Tel: 020 4187 9853.

This action has been taken as part of the National Bank's rationalisation measures.

We regret any inconvenience this closure may cause customers.

Mrs Edith Knowles, Branch Manager

National Bank
Finchley Branch
334 High Road, Finchley
London, N12 8PL
Tel: 020 4655 6233

(today's date)

STAGE 6: CHECK YOUR WORK
CHECKLIST: NOTICES

1	Have you completed the task?	✓
2	Is the layout correct?	✓
3	Have you included a date, and a name and position?	✓
4	Have you given the notice a heading?	✓
5	Have you included all the relevant information?	✓
6	Have you ordered the information in the best way?	✓
7	Is the language appropriate for a notice?	✓
8	Have you checked spelling, grammar and punctuation?	✓

PRACTICE 1

SECTION 3: NOTICES

PART-TIME STAFF WANTED

Are you looking for a part-time job?

Do you want flexible working hours? (max. 14hrs. a week)

Have you got a good telephone voice?

Are you friendly and polite?

Able to work in a busy office?

Can you start immediately?

If you can say yes to all of these we want to talk to you.

Apply in person or ring for an appointment to:
Your name, Office Manager
Blue Star Taxis, 34 King William Street, Aberdeen AB7 1FG
info@bst.co.uk www.bst.co.uk
Tel: 01224 465 988

(today's date)

PRACTICE 2

IMPORTANT NOTICE TO PASSENGERS

Como Airlines wish to inform all passengers about new regulations which have come into effect recently.

LUGGAGE
For your own safety the amount of luggage that passengers can take on the aircraft is limited to;
Economy Class - a maximum of 20kg First Class – a maximum of 40kg
Hand Luggage - Each passenger may carry a maximum of 5kg hand luggage

ADDITIONAL ITEMS
Passengers are also allowed to take some small items with them into the cabin, eg magazine, coat, etc, however no sharp or dangerous items are allowed on board.

MEDICINES
Passengers may take on board any medicine which they need during the flight.
Please note: You may need to show a prescription for any medicines.

QUESTIONS
Our staff will ask you questions about your luggage before your flight. These will include questions about who packed your bag and if your bag has been with you at all times. Do not be offended by this. This is their duty and is for your security.

YOUR SAFETY IS OUR HIGHEST PRIORITY.

WE THANK YOU FOR YOUR COOPERATION.

A Candidate
Como Airlines, Via per Cernobbio 28, Como, Italy
(Today's date)

PRACTICE 3

CRUISE INFORMATION

Welcome to SS Titania

MEALS & RESTAURANT
Access to the restaurant is by meal voucher only.
Meal vouchers can be obtained in the restaurant
or from the Information Office on Blue Deck (open throughout journey).

SHOPS ON BOARD
Opening times are from 1700 until 2300 and 0600 until arrival in port.

BARS • LOUNGES • ENTERTAINMENT
Bars are open from embarkation onwards.
The casino operates from 2000 till 0300.
There is live entertainment in the Sunshine Lounge from 1800 till 0100.

FOREIGN EXCHANGE
Full exchange facilities are available at the Exchange Office which is situated next to the Information Office on Blue Deck.

SECURITY
For your own comfort and security we strongly recommend that you lock your cabin door before retiring for the night and that you always keep your cabin door locked when you are not in the cabin.
Valuables can be deposited for safe-keeping at the Information Office.

CUSTOMER SATISFACTION
It is our wish that every customer is completely satisfied during their time with us.
If this is not the case please contact the Information Office at your earliest opportunity.

Your name, Information Officer
SS Titania
(Today's date)

PRACTICE 4

IMPORTANT SAFETY NOTICE

Would all staff make sure they read and implement the following:

1	Don't leave files out on desk.	Put away when you have finished using them.
2	Don't leave anything in aisles.	Put bags/coats, etc. in lockers or under desks.
3	Don't leave drawers/cupboards open.	Close drawers/cupboards when not in use.
4	Don't eat/drink at desk.	Go to staff canteen for meals and snacks.
5	Don't run in the Centre.	Always walk – never run.
6	Don't smoke in the Centre.	Only smoke in the smoking room.

Miss Rosie Hill
Manager
(today's date)

PRACTICE 5

SECTION 3: NOTICES

IMPORTANT NOTICE

RECALL OF SONOPOR VENTURA SR

All Sonopor Ventura SR cars produced between 1st Jan and 1st May are being recalled by the manufacturer.

Owners of cars with serial numbers between FG121-G19-82369 and FG121-G19-99856 should contact Maureen Greene on 01522 986 322 to arrange an appointment to bring their cars in.

This recall is necessary to replace a faulty component in the steering column.

The repair will take approximately 2 hours and is purely a safety precaution.

ALL CARS ARE QUITE SAFE TO DRIVE IN THE MEANTIME.

On behalf of Sonopor I would like to apologise for any inconvenience this may cause.

Tom Bowles
Sales Director
Mill Street Motors

(today's date)

PRACTICE 6

TEMPORARY CLOSURE OF SpaceXpress RIDE

Due to a slight technical problem SpaceXpress will not be in operation this morning.

This action is very much regretted but has been taken in the interests of public safety. Before we re-open the ride it will have to be thoroughly checked by our engineers.

It is hoped that the ride will re-open around lunchtime.

We apologise for any inconvenience this closure may cause.

If in the unlikely event that the ride doesn't open at all today all visitors will be issued with complimentary tickets. Please check at the exits for details before you leave.

Your name, Manager
FutureWorldNow Entertainment Park

(today's date)

YOUR EXAMPLE

SECTION 4: REPORTS

STAGE 1: IDENTIFY THE TASK

Write the report.

STAGE 2: LAYOUT

A report requires a title and the following headings:

1 Terms of Reference
2 Proceedings
3 Findings
4 Conclusions
5 Recommendations

It also requires a signature and a date.

STAGE 3: IDENTIFY RELEVANT INFORMATION

- report for Mrs Cage
- standard of service at 4 restaurants
- visited all 4 restaurants
- Chester – good points/bad points
- Shrewsbury – good points/bad points
- Bristol – good points/bad points
- Cheltenham – good points/bad points
- general opinions
- recommendations

STAGE 4: GROUP/ORDER RELEVANT INFORMATION

Title Standard of Service at Restaurants in Chester, Shrewsbury, Bristol and Cheltenham.

Terms of Reference Mrs Cage has asked for a report on standard of service at the 4 restaurants above.

Proceedings Visited all 4 restaurants. Had something to eat. Observed staff & customers and made notes.

Findings

1 Chester - Service was very good. Friendly, helpful staff. Plates were cleared away quickly and tables were clean. Food served quickly, but not very warm. Staff in general very young, although appeared to be adequately trained.

2 Shrewsbury – Visited on Saturday morning, very busy. Restaurant was full and queues outside door. Staff coping well. No seating available. Problem was customers not leaving after meal, sitting talking at tables. Customers in queue complaining about waiting time.

3 Bristol – Queues outside door. Problem was slow service and uncleared tables. Only 1 employee cleaning up, so customers had to clear their own tables. Told many staff hadn't turned in that day and that this often happened.

4 Cheltenham – Service was good. Food served quickly, but burgers not cooked long enough. Onions missing from my order, cheese tasted like leather. Went to kitchen. Youngsters doing cooking appeared to have no idea.

Conclusions

Standard of service at Chester was good. At Shrewsbury staff were helpful and friendly but restaurant had serious seating problems. Standard of service at Bristol was bad. There is a problem with staff absenteeism. Standard of service at Cheltenham was good, however food was not properly cooked and did not taste very good.

Recommendations

1 All kitchen staff attend a training programme to ensure that food is properly cooked.
2 Instructions given to all staff (particularly Shrewsbury) in how to deal with customers who do not leave.
3 A separate report is commissioned on staff absenteeism at Bristol.

STAGE 5: WRITE THE REPORT

SECTION 4: REPORTS

The Standard of Service at Restaurants in Chester, Shrewsbury, Bristol and Cheltenham

Terms of Reference
Mrs Ann Cage, Managing Director, has asked me to write a report on the standard of service at Burger Express restaurants in Chester, Shrewsbury, Bristol and Cheltenham.

Proceedings
I visited all 4 restaurants and ordered something to eat and drink. I observed staff and customers and made notes.

Findings
1 Chester The service was good and the staff were pleasant and very helpful. Dirty plates were cleared away quickly and all the tables were kept clean. The food was served quickly but was not very warm. In general the staff were very young, although they appeared to be adequately trained.
2 Shrewsbury I visited the Shrewsbury restaurant on a Saturday morning. The restaurant was full and it was extremely busy, although staff appeared to be coping well. People were queuing outside the door because there were no available seats inside. The problem was that customers were not leaving after their meal, and were sitting talking at the tables. People waiting in the queue made several complaints about the waiting time.
3 Bristol When I arrived at the restaurant there were queues outside the door. Here the problem was slow service and uncleared tables. There was only one employee cleaning up and customers had to clear their own tables. When I asked about this I was told that many staff hadn't come to work that day and that this had happened on many occasions before.
4 Cheltenham The service was good and the food was served quickly. However, the burger I ordered had not been cooked properly and was still red inside, the onions were missing and the cheese tasted more like leather than cheese. When I went into the kitchen, all the staff doing the cooking were very young and did not appear to have much idea.

Conclusions
The standard of service at the Chester restaurant was good. The standard of service at the other three restaurants was not satisfactory, even though staff were generally helpful. The Shrewsbury restaurant has serious seating problems for its customers. The Bristol restaurant appears to have a problem with staff absenteeism. At Cheltenham the food was not properly cooked.

Recommendations
1 All kitchen staff attend a training programme to ensure that the food they serve is properly cooked.
2 All staff, particularly at Shrewsbury, are given instructions in how to deal with customers who do not leave.
3 A separate report is commissioned on the issue of staff absenteeism at the Bristol restaurant.

Your name
Date

STAGE 6: CHECK YOUR WORK

CHECKLIST: REPORTS

1	Have you completed the task?	✓
2	Is the layout correct?	✓
3	Does the title tell you briefly what the report is about?	✓
4	Are the headings correct and in the correct order?	✓
5	Have you included the correct information under the correct heading?	✓
6	Have you signed and dated it?	✓
7	Is the language appropriate for a report?	✓
8	Have you checked spelling, grammar and punctuation?	✓

PRACTICE 1

Reasons for Decreasing Sales at AG Shop, Edinburgh

Terms of Reference
Mr Andrew Sheringham, Regional Manager, has asked me to write a report on the reasons for the decrease in sales at the AG Shop in the Waverley Shopping Centre, Edinburgh.

Proceedings
I have compared sales figures for the same period last year and have also spoken to other shop owners and customers.

Findings
1 The strong pound. This has had a major effect on the number of foreign tourists visiting Edinburgh. This is particularly clear in the fall in sales of our Celtic designs, which have always been popular with tourists from mainland Europe. The number of American tourists is down almost 40% on last year. American tourists have always been important as they buy our jewellery at tax-free prices and last year made up 15% of total sales.

2 The shop location. This has been affected by the closure of neighbouring shops to the left and to the right. This makes a bad impression and many people just walk past.

3 Shoplifting. Over the last 6 months there has been a major increase in shoplifting by school children. The girls, mostly aged between 14 and 17, come in groups of up to 10, so it is difficult to observe them all at the same time. This shoplifting is costing the shop a lot of money.

4 No Sales/Discounts. Many customers have requested a sale or have asked for discounts. Our company policy is 'no sales, no discounts.' When customers are told this they go to other shops, which have sales or offer discounts.

Conclusions
The decrease in sales is a result of 3 factors:
1 Fewer people are coming into the shop. There are fewer tourists from abroad and many people just walk past.
2 There has been a significant increase in stock lost due to shoplifting.
3 Many customers have been lost because of company 'no sales, no discount' policy.

Recommendations
I recommend that we:
1 Install a video camera in the shop to prevent shoplifting.
2 Change company policy on sales and discounts.

Your name
Date

PRACTICE 2

SECTION 4: REPORTS

Possible Merger between Pylo Plastics and Penn Plastics Inc

Terms of Reference
The Board of Directors have commissioned this report to find out how their employees would feel about a merger between Pylo Plastics and Penn Plastics Inc.

Proceedings
I spoke to all Department Heads individually and to staff in groups during their lunchbreaks in the staff canteen.

Findings
1 Everyone is unclear as to the effects of a merger.

2 Staff are confused as to whether it is a merger or a takeover.

3 Heads of Departments are not sure how a merger could work.

4 Many employees are worried that the merger will mean job losses, voluntary redundancies, or the closure of the Pylo Plastics factory. They are also worried that they will be transferred to other plants as staff know that Penn Plastics already has 2 factories in the UK.

5 There is also concern as to whether management will be changed and Head Office moved to the US.

6 Staff are unsure as to whether they will be consulted before the merger.

Conclusions
In general there is a lot of uncertainty about the merger. Staff and Department Heads are very worried about possible job losses, factory closure and major changes in the current structure of the company.

Recommendations
I recommend that a memo is sent to all staff and Department Heads explaining what the merger would mean for the company and its employees and informing staff whether they will be consulted or not.

Your name
Date

PRACTICE 3

Suitability of Roundtree Conference Centre

Terms of Reference
Mr Gary Hayes, Sales Director, has asked me to write a report on the suitability of the Roundtree Conference Centre for future conferences and training seminars.

Proceedings
I spent 3 days at a sales conference at Roundtree Conference Centre. During my stay I made my own impressions and talked to staff.

Findings
1 All accommodation rooms were en-suite and had tea/coffee making facilities, TV and air-conditioning.

2 In the Highgrove conference room the tables were arranged very effectively in a U-shape. Table arrangement, however, is flexible. The room was light and all equipment worked well. The acoustics were good although the seats were not very comfortable, and the staff were not very helpful when I mentioned this. The centre has three other similar conference rooms for groups of various sizes.

3 The food was very good offering lots of variety and there was a healthy choice menu.

4 The Relaxation Centre was well-equipped but it was not really large enough in the busy early evening period.

Conclusions
In general the facilities were satisfactory apart from the uncomfortable chairs in the conference room and the Relaxation Centre, which was too busy in the early evening.

Recommendations
I recommend that we use the Centre again but make sure that more comfortable chairs are provided.

Your name
Date

PRACTICE 4

SECTION 4: REPORTS

CONFIDENTIAL

REPORT ON JAKE SINCLAIR AND BARRY BREWSTER

Terms of Reference
Ms Katy Dixon, the Personnel Manager, has asked for a report on Jake Sinclair and Barry Brewster, the two staff who are working a one-month trial period.

Proceedings
Jake Sinclair and Barry Brewster have been working directly under my supervision since they started on Monday 3 September. This report is based on my experience with them and comments from colleagues and customers.

Findings

1 Jake Sinclair and Barry Brewster have been punctual every day.

2 Both are ready to start at 9am and keen to stay on after 5pm if required.

3 Both are well-dressed and get on well with colleagues.

4 Barry Brewster is 18 months younger than Jake Sinclair.

5 Jake Sinclair is more outgoing than Barry Brewster. When talking to customers Barry chooses his words more carefully and if he can't answer a question he will say so and then find out the answer. Jake Sinclair, on the other hand, just keeps on talking.

Conclusions
Both Jake Sinclair and Barry Brewster have made a good impression with customers, colleagues and myself. They have both been reliable and smart. They have different characters but both have good points.

Recommendations
I recommend Barry Brewster as I think he will become more self-confident over time and will give customers accurate information.

Your name
Date

PRACTICE 5

ACCIDENT INVOLVING MR WILFRED SMITH

Terms of Reference
Sir Humphrey McAulay, MD, has asked me to write a report about the recent accident at the Central Warehouse in Exeter involving Mr Wilfred Smith and a fork-lift truck.

Proceedings
I visited the Exeter Warehouse, checked the accident report card and spoke to staff who were present at the time of the accident.

Findings
1 The accident happened on 14 April at 6.45pm when Wilfred Smith was hit by a fork-lift truck driven by Henry Stevens. As a result of this he broke his right leg in two places. An ambulance was called immediately and he was taken to Exeter General Hospital.

2 Arthur Smedley was working with Wilfred Smith when the accident happened. He said that both himself and Wilfred Smith should have finished work at 6pm and were hurrying to get finished. Wilfred Smith had been hurrying down the main passage and turned into passage 3b just as the fork-lift truck was reversing out. It appears that Wilfred Smith walked into the fork-lift truck rather than the other way around. The driver had no chance to stop.

3 The Warehouse Manager confirmed that all staff were working overtime because 4 employees were off ill. He added that all staff working in the warehouse are new and that none of them have been with the company for longer than 6 weeks. He confirmed that none of the staff had received any safety training and that this was because there had been no time. He also commented that staff turnover was very high and the reason for this was that the job is not very well paid.

Conclusions
The accident appears to have been a result of employees not being aware of basic safety procedures.

Recommendations
I recommend that all staff attend a one-day safety training course during their first week of employment. This should be followed by further training sessions held every six months. In order to reduce staff turnover the pay scale for warehouse staff should be reviewed.

Your name
Date

PRACTICE 6 SECTION 4: REPORTS

INCREASE IN PAPER USE

Terms of Reference
Mrs Gerard, Financial Director, has asked me to write a report on the increase in the amount of paper being used.

Proceedings
I checked with accounts to see how much paper had been bought and then spoke to staff and management to find out reasons for the increase.

Findings
Our costs for paper have tripled in the last 6 months. This is as a result of the following:

1 E-Mails. There has been a large increase in the number of e-mails sent and received. These messages are sometimes one word long and other times are several pages long. Staff print out every message sent and received, irrespective of length.

2 Printers. Faster printers make it much easier and quicker to print out documents. Employees don't check their work on screen. They print it out, then correct it and print it out again - sometimes up to 4 times before they have the final version. Most of these print outs are thrown into the wastepaper bin.

3 Internet. Many employees now find information on the internet. When they find useful websites they print out web pages, many of which are later thrown away.

4 Filing. Many staff, and young staff in particular, don't like filing documents. They find it easier and faster to print documents out every time they need them and then throw them away.

Conclusions
In general there is a huge amount of paper wastage, which is mainly due to laziness and carelessness on the part of staff.

Recommendations
I recommend that guidelines are produced and issued to all staff concerning e-mail use, checking work on screen, internet use and filing of documents with a view to making staff more aware of how to avoid excessive use of paper.

Your name
Date

YOUR EXAMPLE

SECTION 5: ARTICLES

STAGE 1: IDENTIFY THE TASK
Write the article.

STAGE 2: LAYOUT
The article requires a title, an arresting opening, a middle and an ending.

STAGE 3: IDENTIFY RELEVANT INFORMATION
- AEC established 1989
- electricity to over 500,000 homes and businesses
- anniversary of visitor centre / opened last June
- already over 30,000 visitors
- opening times
- free entry to exhibitions & displays
- ideal for children, school parties, family days out
- exhibition, model, display, etc
- awards for design (The New Building Award from the CBI)
- newspapers quotes

STAGE 4: GROUP/ORDER RELEVANT INFORMATION
1 AEC established 1989.
2 Electricity to over 500,000 homes and businesses.
3 Anniversary of visitor centre - opened last June. Already had over 30,000 visitors.
4 Centre has won awards for design (The New Building Award from the CBI).
5 "Very important architectural project" (Daily News).
6 Exhibitions & displays.
7 "Very entertaining and educational" (Morning Star).
8 "The exhibitions were simply fascinating" (The Courier).
9 Ideal for children, school parties, family days out.
10 'Moving Water' exhibition, Model of power station, 'Power of Water' display, etc.
11 Open 7 days, 10am - 8pm. Closed bank holidays. Free entry.

STAGE 5: WRITE THE ARTICLE

AEC's Visitor Centre celebrates first anniversary

Welcome to AEC Hydroelectric plc, established in 1989 and bringing electricity to over 500,000 homes and business throughout the country.

This month sees the first anniversary of AEC's Visitor Centre, which has been visited and enjoyed by more than 30,000 visitors since opening last June.

To date the Centre has received numerous awards for its design, most notably "The New Building Award" from the CBI. The press has been equally kind, the Daily News referring to it as a "Very important architectural project".

During the year AEC's Visitor Centre has staged a succession of exhibitions and displays which have won universal praise. The Morning Star found them "Very entertaining and educational" and The Courier delighted to announce "The exhibitions were simply fascinating".

Whether just for all the family on a day out or for a school party AEC's Visitor Centre is the ideal place for children. Here they can enjoy the hands-on 'Moving Water' exhibition, study a scale model of the power station or marvel at the 'Power of Water' display as well as many other attractions.

AEC's Visitor Centre is open, 10am till 8pm, seven days a week, excluding bank holidays and admission is free, so come along and see what it's all about.

PRACTICE 1

SECTION 5: ARTICLES

VTR's guide to Spain

You may be asked to go to Spain on behalf of the company, but would you know what to do when you get there?

Perhaps because of the climate Spaniards tend to start work later in the morning and work till later at night than in the UK. Businesses are usually open from 0930 until 1330 and from 1630 until 2030 with a "siesta" from 1330 until 1630.

Banks are open for business from 0830 until 1430 Monday through Saturday, except in summer when they are closed on Saturday.

There are no special norms in Spain with regard to dress at work. From a practical point of view lightweight clothes are better because of the climate. A lightweight suit, short-sleeved shirt and tie is ideal for work. It is not necessary to dress formally for dinner - smart casual clothes are perfectly adequate.

Restaurant hours are varied. Bars are usually open all day and close late at night.

Tipping is a great tradition in Spain. Almost all places include a charge for services in the bill but it is still common to tip as well. 5% to 10% is normal. This is common in bars and restaurants and also for taxi drivers.

So, if you are asked to go, at least you now know the basics.

PRACTICE 2

DIDA Publishing House – your partner for the Czech Republic

Founded in Prague in 1993, DIDA Educational Publishing House has specialised from the beginning in the production of textbooks and resource material for teachers as well as self-study workbooks for students.

Our books are sold throughout the Czech Republic and users value them highly.

We print books under licence and distribute books for foreign publishers in the Czech Republic through a chain of bookshops in 30 towns and cities. We also supply to many other bookshops in the Czech Republic.

In 1996 a sister company DIDA Warsaw, was established in Poland. It too is orientated towards publishing, distributing and printing under licence. Both companies cooperate extensively, providing extra benefit for foreign publishers.

So if you are looking for a partner in the Czech Republic who has the best contacts and the necessary know-how why don't you visit us in Hall 3 Stand 456 where Eva and Paul will be pleased to discuss your needs.

PRACTICE 3

It's Rita's 40th year!

At 16 years of age Rita Powell left school and walked straight into a job with Glasden Chemicals. She has been with the company ever since. Now, 40 years on and working in the Wages Department, she remains one of our company's most loyal employees.

In the last 40 years Rita has seen lots of changes take place in the industry where she has progressed from working completely by hand to working with the latest technology. According to Rita one of the reasons why the job has remained so interesting is the fact that she has constantly had to learn new methods and to use new equipment.

To mark her incredible service to the company, colleagues both old and new, joined her in a presentation on the factory floor, where she received many gifts including a gold clock as a token of all our gratitude.

Well done Rita!

PRACTICE 4

Official Opening a Great Success - Thanks to Staff

Congratulations to all members of staff for your support at the official opening of Ringway House. It will certainly be remembered for a long time and was a very special day in the company's history.

Friday 27th April saw the Main Hall taken over by a staged area decorated in our company's corporate colours featuring a multi-screen powerpoint display showing examples of the type of work our company carries out.

The fact that we were able to host the event in the centre of a working environment was one of the things which really impressed our visitors.

Chairman, Bill Shed, officially welcomed the visitors amongst whom were many distinguished guests from the business community.

After the more formal proceedings, visitors were invited to take a guided tour around Ringway House. On view was the very latest technology in use in the printing industry today.

Thank you again to all staff without whom this memorable day would not have been possible.

PRACTICE 5

SECTION 5: ARTICLES

A Year in Geneva

The thought of going abroad for a year made me feel as though I was a 1st year student again. I had to make new friends, find my way about in a new city, get used to the university and above all get used to living in a different country.

The reason I went to Geneva was because I was studying International Management in London and a requirement of the course is that every student has to spend one year in a different country in order to gain international experience.

Switzerland was for me the obvious choice. I had visited the country many times before and was curious to see what it would be like to actually live there. Another reason was that I spoke some "school" French. The course was excellent and I learnt a lot about international management, international marketing and exports, which were the main subjects I studied.

My time in Geneva taught me a lot academically but it also gave me the chance to get inside another culture and my French has improved greatly.

In short, it was an experience that I was glad to have had the chance of.

PRACTICE 6

A First-Class Workforce

Wills Electronics is continuing to make employee development a top priority, having invested more than £7 million in training and development programmes over the past year.

Employees at all levels of Wills Electronics – from trainees to senior managers – are benefiting from these programmes.

Around 250 trainees, aged under 18, are currently on a special two-year programme which allows them to learn the key aspects of their jobs and gain an accredited qualification before taking up their position within the company.

In addition graduates are being recruited for a management training scheme and support is also given to apprentice engineers through work placements.

Investment in further education is currently supporting 350 staff in a variety of training and language courses.

If you are interested in enrolling on any of the training courses offered by the company either speak to your Department Manager or contact Mrs Bell on Ext. 890. Details of all the courses on offer are posted on the noticeboard in the staff canteen.

YOUR EXAMPLE

SECTION 6: LISTS

STAGE 1: IDENTIFY THE TASK

Write the list.

STAGE 2: LAYOUT

A list requires a title and numbered points.

STAGE 3: IDENTIFY RELEVANT INFORMATION

- use only for intended purpose
- read manual before operating
- door interlock for safety
  - door won't open when in use
  - don't force door, wait a minute
- don't put flammable garments (cleaning sprays / liquids) in machine
- coins / metal objects can damage drum
- don't wash heavy items alone (bath mats, cotton sheets, towels)
  - wash in a balanced load
- remove dispensers for washing powder etc before tumble drying
- foam and rubber articles not suitable for tumble dryer - don't put in
- drum gets hot during tumble drying
  - allow the dryer to complete cool down period
  - then remove washing
- cold water supply must be turned on for tumble drying
- if machine is faulty stop using it
- after use turn off water supply
- remove plug from electricity supply

STAGE 4: GROUP/ORDER RELEVANT INFORMATION

<u>DO</u>

1 Only use for intended purpose.
2 Read manual before operating.
3 Wait a minute if door won't open, then try again - machine has a doorlocking safety feature.
4 Remove all dispensers for washing powder etc before tumble drying.
5 Allow dryer to complete cool down period before removing washing - the drum gets very hot.
6 Make sure cold water supply is turned on when tumble drying.
7 Make sure you turn off water supply after use.
8 Always take plug out of electricity supply after use.

<u>DON'T</u>

1 Don't force door open if there is water in drum or drum is still turning.
2 Don't put flammable garments in machine (eg cleaning sprays / liquids).
3 Don't put coins or metal objects in machine - can damage drum.
4 Don't wash heavy items alone (eg bath mats, cotton sheets, towels) - wash in a balanced load.
5 Don't put foam and rubber articles in dryer - they are not suitable.
6 Don't use the machine if it appears to be faulty.

SECTION 6: LISTS

STAGE 5: WRITE THE LIST

INSTRUCTIONS FOR WASHER/DRYER 1200 X456

DO

1 Only use for the intended purpose.

2 Read the manual before operating.

3 Wait a minute if door won't open, then try again
- the machine has a doorlocking safety feature.

4 Remove all dispensers for washing powder etc before tumble drying.

5 Allow dryer to complete cool down period before removing your washing
- the drum gets very hot when in use.

6 Make sure that the cold water supply is turned on when tumble drying.

7 Make sure you turn off water supply after use.

8 Always take the plug out of the electricity supply after use.

DON'T

1 Don't force the door if it doesn't open
- there is still water in the drum or the drum is still turning.

2 Don't put flammable garments in the machine
- eg garments treated with cleaning sprays or flammable liquids.

3 Don't put coins or other small metal objects in - they can damage the drum.

4 Don't wash heavy items on their own - always wash in a balanced load
- eg bath mats, cotton sheets, towels.

5 Don't put foam and rubber articles in the dryer - they are not suitable.

6 Don't continue to use the machine if it appears to be faulty.

STAGE 6: CHECK YOUR WORK

CHECKLIST: LISTS

1	Have you completed the task?	✓
2	Is the layout correct?	✓
3	Have you given the list a title?	✓
4	Have you used numbered points and headings if appropriate?	✓
5	Have you included all the relevant information?	✓
6	Have you ordered the information in the best way?	✓
7	Is the language appropriate for a list?	✓
8	Have you checked spelling, grammar and punctuation?	✓

PRACTICE 1

DAL FIRE EXTINGUISHERS

1 DAL FIRE EXTINGUISHERS

- manufactured to high specification
- first class protection
- guaranteed performance
- refillable
- pressure gauge shows serviceability
- read instructions carefully when you buy
- annual inspection recommended

2 EXTINGUISHERS AT HOME

- easy to see
- easy to reach

DAL recommend

- hallway
- landing
- kitchen
- one on each floor

3 EXTINGUISHERS IN CARS

- accessible for occupants
- not in car boot
- not where restricted access
- fix firmly to avoid injury in accident

In the event of fire

1. Stop vehicle in the safest possible position.
2. Turn off ignition.
3. Get out of vehicle.
4. Call the Fire Brigade.
5. Stand back if the fire is intense.

If fire in engine compartment

1. Open bonnet as far as safety catch.
2. Point extinguisher through gap.
3. Don’t open bonnet fully.

PRACTICE 2

SECTION 6: LISTS

10th LINGUAMARKT INTERNATIONAL LANGUAGE FAIR

1 Linguamarkt is the largest language fair in Germany and is now in its 10th year.

2 The venue is Stuttgart Conference and Exhibition Centre.

3 The main theme is the future language requirements of European business.

4 Over 200 exhibitors from 30 countries will have stands at the fair.

5 Providers of language courses, qualifications and examinations will be present.

6 Publishers will display language-related teaching materials, literature and dictionaries.

7 Software and multimedia products will be exhibited.

8 Future generations will need to learn languages.

9 Language skills will be necessary for careers and jobs in a global market.

10 Peaceful cooperation between nations will depend on knowledge of languages.

11 Learning languages is a life-long obligation for everybody.

PRACTICE 3

ELEC FRIDGE FREEZERS

GENERAL POINTS

- two compressors
- independent thermostat controls for fridge & freezer
- most advanced cooling and freezing technology
- newest innovations for food safety
- designed for simplicity of use
- easy to operate control panels
- fast freeze switch
- temperature warning light

SPECIAL FEATURES

1 **Specially designed doors**
- cover dairy compartment
- prevent foods picking up other flavours

2 **Butter dish and egg trays**
- in most models

3 **Glass shelves**
- stable nonslip surface
- ensure no cross contamination of foods

4 **Tall bottle flap**
- allows for upright storage of large bottles

5 **Tilting upper shelf**
- keeps corks wet when chilling wine

6 **Meat/salad box**
- hygienic storage
- unique reversible lid
- seals for storing salad
- allows ventilation for storing meat

7 **Salad compartments**
- long-lasting plastic drawers
- two drawer fruit and vegetable store

8 **Freezer**
- designed to prevent cold air escaping when door is open
- special holder on door for useful advice on home freezing

PRACTICE 4

SECTION 6: LISTS

TRAVEL INSURANCE

Major providers are travel agents and tour operators.

NEW RESEARCH

- consumers now know more
- demanding lower prices & higher levels of service
- premiums can vary by up to 50% for same cover
- annual insurance more popular as people travel more frequently
- increased 500% in last 2 years
- 1 in 6 buy direct from insurance company

KEY FEATURES

1 **HOLIDAY INSURANCE COVER**

- insurance against cancellation of holiday
- medical cover at least £1m for travel in Europe
- medical cover of £2m outside Europe

2 **PERSONAL LIABILITY INSURANCE**

- essential in US (lawsuit costs can bankrupt you)
- entry can be refused if less than £2 million cover

3 **BAGGAGE**

- cover for lost, stolen, damaged baggage
- **"first needs"** until luggage forwarded

4 **MONEY & VALUABLES**

- sometimes excluded from cover to keep premiums down
- necessary if your valuables are stolen

PRACTICE 5

INCREASE IN OBESITY RATES

1 OBESITY RATES

The number of overweight people worldwide equals the number of underfed people.

- 1.2 billion obese adults
- 1.2 billion underfed adults

(statistics from US based research organisation)

2 GLOBAL TREND

Not just Western Europe but poorer countries as well.
Populations are moving from country to a sedentary city life.

Britain

- 50% of adults are too fat
- obesity rates doubled in last 10 years

Latin American

Brazil
- 31% of population overweight

Columbia
- 43% of population overweight

Great poverty in countryside in both countries

China

- 15% of population overweight in 1990's (9% in 1980's)
  - traditional diet
    - healthy
    - non-dairy
    - vegetable-based diet

3 TREATING OBESITY-RELATED ILLNESSES

The costs in Britain are £2 billion a year (6% of national health budget).

Government

- has done little to curb the problem
- abandoned targets to reduce obesity 10 years ago

4 CHANGING THE TREND

- increase exercise dramatically
- encourage people to do this
- no longer enough simply to walk instead of drive
- need to encourage people to participate in sports

PRACTICE 6

SECTION 6: LISTS

TELEPHONE ETIQUETTE

The way in which a telephone call is answered creates a lasting impression.

It is important for a firm to plan guidelines on how to answer calls:

1. Answer quickly

This is a sign that your business is efficient

- Aim to answer within 2 rings
- More than 3 rings is unacceptable; callers feel unimportant and angry

2. Speak slowly

Always speak slowly and clearly

Speaking quickly shows of lack of interest

3. Welcome callers

Thank the caller for calling

State the name of the firm clearly

Give your name

Ask how you can help

Be helpful

Using the telephone properly is a simple way to keep your customers happy.

YOUR EXAMPLE SECTION 7: LETTERS

STAGE 1: IDENTIFY THE TASK

Write the letter.

STAGE 2: LAYOUT

Sender's address:	77 – 81 Bridge Street, Formby, Liverpool, L37 7WE
Recipient's name:	GJFC C/o Mr Ian Pearson
Recipient's address:	24 Ashby Road, Manchester, M14 3HS
Appropriate date:	2 August …
Correct salutation:	Dear Mr Pearson
Correct complimentary close:	Yours sincerely
Sender's signature:	(your signature)
Sender's name:	(your name)
Sender's position:	Sales Assistant

STAGE 3: IDENTIFY RELEVANT INFORMATION

- thanks for letter
- available flights
  - 22 people
  - Manchester – Paris
  - 1 September (am)
  - 0615, £48, no discounts
- available flights
  - 22 people
  - Paris – Manchester
  - 21 September (pm)
  - 1335, £49, no discounts
  - 1500, £128, 40% discount for under 16's
  - 1630, £99, 30% discount for under 16's
- fares and discounts for under 16's
- booking terms and conditions
  - no cancellation once booked – no refunds
  - 20% deposit payable when customer confirms
  - remainder 14 days before travel
- hotel details
  - suggest website www.sporthotel.com
  - call into shop

STAGE 4: GROUP/ORDER RELEVANT INFORMATION

1 Thanks for letter.

2 Available flights Manchester – Paris
- 22 people on 1 September (am) / fares & discounts
- one flight.

3 Available flights Paris - Manchester
- 22 people on 21 September (pm) / fares & discounts
- choice of flights.

4 Booking terms and conditions.

5 Hotel – suggest website.

SECTION 7: LETTERS

STAGE 5: WRITE THE LETTER

ACE Worldwide Travel
77 – 81 Bridge Street, Formby, Liverpool, L37 7WE
Tel: 01704 221 6594

Greenwood Juniors Football Club
C/o Mr Ian Pearson
24 Ashby Road
Manchester
M14 3HS

2 August …

Dear Mr Pearson

Thank you for your letter of 29 July. We have checked the available flights for the dates you requested.

On the morning of the 1 September there is only one flight for Paris which has 22 seats available. This flight leaves Manchester at 0615 and the tickets are £48 per person. There is no discount for under 16's.

On the afternoon of 21 September there is a choice of flights from Paris to Manchester. The cheapest flight leaves Paris at 1335. The tickets are £49 with no discount for under 16's. If you would prefer a later flight there is a flight at 1630 (price £99 with 30% discount for under 16's) or a flight at 1500 (price £128 with 40% discount for under 16's).

Please let me know if you wish to book these flights. Once flights are booked they can't be cancelled and we can't offer any refunds. We require 20% deposit payable when you confirm the booking and the remainder 14 days before the date of travel.

We recommend that you visit the website sporthotel.com to find a suitable hotel for your needs. If you don't have internet access please call in to the shop where we can visit their website and show you other possible hotels in Paris.

Yours sincerely

(your signature)

(your name)
Sales Assistant

STAGE 6: CHECK YOUR WORK

CHECKLIST: LETTERS

1	Have you completed the task?	✓
2	Is the layout correct?	✓
3	Are the sender's details and the recipient's details correct?	✓
4	Is the date appropriate?	✓
5	Have you included all the relevant information?	✓
6	Have you ordered the information in the best way?	✓
7	Is the language appropriate for a letter?	✓
8	Have you checked spelling, grammar and punctuation?	✓

PRACTICE 1

Tel: 0161 764 5896

Smith's Transport
Unit 350
Glenfield Industrial Estate
Bury
Lancashire
BL8 5DX

Mr John Brown
Coolit Ltd
22 Wardle Business Park
King's Street
Knutsford
Cheshire
WA16 6JD

28 April …

Dear Mr Brown

Thank you for your letter of 24 April which I have read with interest.

Smith's Transport is a haulage contractor specialising in the transport of frozen goods. We have a fleet of over 70 refrigerated lorries and carry out daily deliveries to all parts of the UK. We also have facilities for storing frozen foodstuffs if these are needed now or in the future. We have a huge amount of experience in this field and believe that we would be the ideal partner to supply your transport requirements.

In order to gain an exact idea of your needs I suggest a meeting and would be pleased to visit you to discuss details.

I look forward to hearing from you.

Yours sincerely

Brian Ferguson
Transport Manager

PRACTICE 2

SECTION 7: LETTERS

Westbank Hotel and Conference Centre
23 – 25 New Mount Street, Bath, Avon, BA1 8DF
Tel: 01225 456 666 Fax: 01225 456 600
E-mail info@westbankhotel.co.uk Website: www.westbankhotel.co.uk

Solpro Properties
Miss Zoe Henry
44 Marylands Avenue
New Romney
Kent
TN28 8FR

16 August …

Dear Miss Henry

Thank you for your letter of 12 August.

We are very pleased that you are considering Westbank Hotel and Conference Centre for your annual sales conference.

We are able to accommodate up to 100 delegates on the dates you require and have suitable conference suites available. The Mendip Conference Room is designed for 90 delegates and is available during the day on all 3 days requested. If there are more than 90 delegates we can offer the Cotswold Conference Room, which holds 110 people, for the first two days and the Stowe Conference Room, which holds 140 people, for the final day.

All of our conference rooms have excellent acoustics and refreshments are included in the price. The hotel has recently completed a programme of improvements including wheelchair access to all accommodation and conference rooms, and the installation of a relaxation centre with swimming pool, sauna, solarium and steambath, which is open every day from 1pm to 10pm.

I have enclosed a brochure and current price list. We would need to have confirmation of the number of delegates by 15 September and would also need to know if the vegetarians eat fish and eggs or not.

Please do not hesitate to contact me to discuss any more details.

Yours sincerely

Esther Woodford (Mrs)
Manager

PRACTICE 3

Great Southern Railways
30 – 32 Church Road, Treganna, St Ives, Cornwall, TR6 8BB
Tel: 01736 799 541 Fax: 01736 785 255
Website: ***www.**gst.co.uk* Email: *info@gst.co.uk*

Mrs Janet Mills
47 Holland Street
London
SE1 9KL

16 September …

Dear Mrs Mills

Thank you for your letter of 13 September.

I apologise for the inexcusable delays which you experienced on 8 September and for the resulting cancellation of your meeting with clients.

I have checked the situation and have been informed that the train left the station one hour late because of a bomb hoax. It was decided not to give any information to the public to avoid passengers panicking. Whilst I understand your dissatisfaction at not being told of the situation I am sure you can understand why we decided it was in the best interest of the public not to inform them of the situation in this case. Security and the safety of our passengers are of the utmost importance to Great Southern Railways and we take every bomb scare seriously.

The further delay of 45 minutes was caused by a signal failure. Passengers should have been informed of this and I can only apologise for the lack of information in this case.

Our normal policy is not to refund money unless trains are cancelled. However, if you have to make the same journey again to see your clients because your meeting was cancelled, we are prepared to exchange your ticket for a new one. Please send me your old ticket and your new date(s) of travel and I will send you a valid ticket.

I apologise for the inconvenience caused and hope that you will understand the situation and continue to travel with Great Southern Railways.

Yours sincerely

(your signature)

(your name)
Customer Services Manager

PRACTICE 4

SECTION 7: LETTERS

GSL International Recruitment Agency
17 Quai d'Orsay, F-75007 Paris
Tel: 33/1 40 62 55 41 Fax: 33/1 40 62 56 92
W: *www.gsl-recruiting.fr*
E: *info@gsl-recruiting.fr*

Auton Software
Dr Jonathan Wright
Unit 19
Business Square
Great Guildford Street
London
SE1 0HS
United Kingdom

16 January …

Dear Dr Wright

Thank you for your letter of 12 January regarding the recruitment of a sales person for your company in France.

We have checked our files and recommend Mr Thierry Meyer for the position. He speaks fluent French and English (also German). He has a degree in Business Studies, has worked as a Sales Representative for a software company and also as a Financial Manager. He has excellent computer skills and has a full driving licence. A copy of his CV is enclosed.

If you are in agreement with our choice of candidate we will arrange an interview with him in our rooms in Paris. Please let us know what dates would be suitable for you.

If you would like us to arrange other candidates to attend interviews at the same time please let us know as we have several other candidates who have most of the requirements for the position with your company.

I look forward to hearing from you.

Yours sincerely

Alain Saille (Mr)
Manager

PRACTICE 5

Global Office Supplies
PO Box 340, Borehamwood, Herts WD6 1LT
Tel: 020 2369 5846 Fax: 020 2369 5700
Website: www.globaloffice.com
Email: sales@globaloffice.com

Mr Patrick Rhodes
Director
Wiseman Medical Supplies
56 Eldon Road
Leith
Edinburgh
EH1 3WP

26 January …

Dear Mr Rhodes

I have made enquiries concerning the mistakes, which you mention in your letter of 22 January. Over the last 2 weeks many staff have been off work due to the flu epidemic. In order to fulfil customers' orders staff who were not ill had to work long hours and overtime to cover for the staff who were off sick.

The errors on your invoice were made by a temporary member of staff, now no longer with us, who did not know that Wiseman Medical Supplies were eligible for a discount and therefore issued an invoice with no discount. A credit note will be issued for the difference.

The labels which were missing from the last delivery have been sent to you by express courier. Please return the packing material which was not requested at our cost.

I apologise for the problems which you have experienced. This is the first time that we have had such problems and I admit that we were unprepared for the situation caused by the flu epidemic. Nearly all of the staff are now back at work and we have taken steps to ensure that such a situation will not happen again.

Yours sincerely

Max Humphreys
Sales Manager

PRACTICE 6

SECTION 7: LETTERS

Adonis Model Agency
Königsallee 15, D-40210 Düsseldorf
Tel: 0211/ 37 64 27 Fax: 0211/ 37 64 0

IT Fashion Magazine
Ms Jancis Morgan
IT House
Edgware
London
NW3 5YH
England

2 June …

Dear Ms Morgan

<u>Interview with Gisele</u>

We were very pleased to receive your letter of 29 May concerning our model, Gisele, and are in agreement with your proposal to interview her for your magazine.

We would be able to hold the interview in our guest apartment in Düsseldorf old town and suggest the afternoon of Thursday 15 June. This would allow you to fly into Düsseldorf and return on the same day.

Please could you confirm that this date is convenient and let me know what time you will arrive so that we can arrange transport for you from the airport.

Please let me know if there is anything in particular which you want to know about Gisele or our agency, so that I can bring all the necessary information with me. We can also discuss the possibility of using her face on the front cover when we meet.

I look forward to hearing from you.

Yours sincerely

Ursula Zimmermann (Mrs)
Agency Manager

ANSWERS

FURTHER PRACTICE

QUESTION	TASK
1	LEAFLET
2	MEMO
3	REPORT
4	LIST
5	ARTICLE
6	NOTICE
7	LETTER
8	NOTICE
9	MEMO
10	ARTICLE
11	LIST
12	REPORT
13	LETTER
14	LEAFLET
15	NOTICE
16	REPORT
17	LEAFLET
18	MEMO
19	LIST
20	LETTER

QUESTION 1 (LEAFLET)

HARTHILL HOUSE MID-SUMMER FAIR

Saturday 21st and Sunday 22nd June
11am – 4pm

Unique opportunity to visit an 11th century country house

FREE ENTRY to house and gardens

Lunches and afternoon teas in the Cottage RESTAURANT

Harthill ales in brewery shop – all at DISCOUNT

Sale of CRAFTS AND ANTIQUES in tent on front lawn

Plants for sale in gardens (various stalls)

HORSE RIDES • BOUNCY CASTLE • HELICOPTER RIDES

Local MUSIC band (Just Red) Sun 1pm

SHEEPDOG DISPLAY Sun 3pm

All enquiries 01586 326 589

Wallingford, Oxfordshire, OX10 7BN. Tel: 01865 256 588
Issued on 5th May

QUESTION 2 (MEMO)

MEMO

To: All staff
From: Mrs Suzanne Hayes
Subject: Leaking of confidential information
Date: Today's date

I have learned that confidential company information has been leaked to the press. As you may know a report recently appeared in a newspaper concerning our new heart disease product. The article contained confidential company information which could only have come from an employee of this company.

I would remind all staff that they must not discuss details about the company or company products with anyone. If you receive enquiries for information pass them on to the company's Press Officer. Be especially careful if you receive unusual telephone calls. Report them immediately to me.

Remember our company's new products are important for the future of the company and leaked information could be of great help to our competitors. This must not happen again.

QUESTION 3 (REPORT)

Implementation of Guidelines for Telephone Operators at Dial-up Bank

Terms of Reference
Mrs Gaby Silver, Customer Services Manager of Dial-up Bank, has commissioned IRS to write a report on whether the new guidelines for telephone operators are being followed.

Proceedings
I called the bank 78 times over a two week period and carried out various tasks, from everyday transactions to very specific enquiries.

Findings
1 90% of the time the phone was answered within 5 rings. On one occasion I had to wait 8 rings before the phone was answered.

2 The name of the operator was given on every occasion. However, I could not always understand the name of the operator and had to ask for the name to be repeated several times.

3 Under half informed me that the call would be recorded. When I asked the operators why it was being recorded, only one could tell me that it was for training and security purposes.

4 Every time I contacted the bank I was asked to give my date of birth and postcode. On 5 occasions I gave the wrong details, and every time was not able to continue until I gave the correct information.

5 I did not encounter any problems when executing simple everyday tasks, such as transferring money or ordering a chequebook. However, when I enquired about exchange rates I was put on hold for 8 minutes and when I was finally given the requested exchange rate it was incorrect. When I tried to transfer money to an account I hold in another country I was passed on to other operators 3 times and eventually the operator hung up.

6 I contacted the bank to complain on 12 occasions. During all but two of these calls, I was transferred to a superior member of staff immediately.

7 There were many times when I called the bank and could not get through because all of the lines were engaged.

Conclusions
Most of the guidelines are being followed by telephone operators, however, the following areas need attention: speaking clearly when giving name, informing customers that the call is recorded and executing unusual tasks.

Recommendations
1 Operators should be instructed to speak clearly when giving their name.

2 Operators should be informed that they must inform callers that the call is being recorded.

3 Some members of staff should be trained to carry out less common tasks, so that all enquiries for these can be transferred to them to deal with.

Your name
Date

QUESTION 4 (LIST)

THE EYECARE ORGANISATION

1	**Eyesight**	• very precious • need - good advice - good care - good treatment • needs to be affordable
2	**Eyecare organisation**	• nationwide organisation • more than 500 opticians in UK • only employ fully qualified staff • professional care • friendly, personal service • national standard of professional care • back-up of a national organisation
3	**Eyecare customers**	• regular eye examinations • advice on eye health and safety • advice on choosing spectacles or contact lenses • information about children's special needs • one year's guarantee against faulty spectacles • value for money

QUESTION 5 (ARTICLE)

Special Delivery service takes market by storm

Launched at the end of last year, "Special Delivery" replaces the former "Next Day Plus" service offered by Express Couriers. Already rated the best for cost, speed and reliability in a recent survey, "Special Delivery" is being chosen by more and more companies who realise that choosing the right courier service makes sound business sense.

Sales to date of "Special Delivery" have shot up by 24% compared to the previous "Next Day Plus" service.

"Special Delivery" guarantees Express Couriers' customers next day delivery by 12 noon anywhere in the UK and special envelopes and containers are provided free of charge.

Jenny Ross, Marketing Manager at Express Couriers, says, "Express Courier's Special Delivery offers a simplified and improved service to our customers as well as a more effective and reliable service than anything our competitors can offer."

QUESTION 6 (NOTICE)

TEMPORARY CLOSURE OF RECEPTION AREA

We regret that the reception area will be closed today due to a leaking roof.
This has been caused by the recent severe storms.
Workmen are repairing the roof and the reception area will be open as usual tomorrow.
In the meantime it is "Business as Usual" and we would advise all customers to please use the side entrance in South Street.
We apologise for any inconvenience caused.

Your name, Owner
RJS Photographic Studio
(today's date)

QUESTION 7 (LETTER)

Tel: 01392 426 255

PLT Cinema
9 King's Road
Exeter
EX5 4HG

MCME
Miss Michelle George
Managing Director
Chatham
Kent
TN14 7TG

27 March …

Dear Miss George

JAMES THOMSON

James Thomson was employed by PLT Cinema from June 1994 until December 1999. During this period he worked his way up from Assistant Cinematographer, to Chief Cinematographer and finally to Assistant Manager. He left PLT to work as Promotional Manager for a larger cinema company. This gave him the contact with people which he enjoyed so much. While he worked at PLT he was always well-dressed, punctual and reliable. He had excellent people skills and was a good communicator. He was also well-liked and respected by staff and management.

He was an excellent employee, an asset to the company and I have no hesitation in recommending him for the job for which he has applied.

Please do not hesitate to contact me if you require any more information.

Yours sincerely

Hugh Phillips
Managing Director

QUESTION 8 (NOTICE)

UNDER NEW MANAGEMENT

To celebrate the re-opening of the Mayflower Restaurant
we would like to make you an offer you cannot refuse.

Our new dinner menu available during the month of November offers you a superb
15% discount off the entire bill.
(This includes drinks and wine.)

To book, simply telephone the Restaurant on (01596) 986 555.

The Restaurant is open for Dinner
Thursday to Saturday from 7pm till 9pm
Booking is essential.

We also serve
All-Day Snacks, Lunches and Coffee
10am till 4pm Monday to Sunday.

Your name, Owner
Mayflower Restaurant
6 Highgate, Taunton, TN7 6PW
(today's date)

QUESTION 9 (MEMO)

MEMO

To: All staff
From: Your name, MD
Subject: Japanese export order
Date: Today's date

As you probably know we have just won a major export order to Japan, which will be very important for the future of this company. The order was won as a result of long and difficult negotiations, which were finally completed when the Japanese delegation spent three days here in the factory. I am sure that the reception they received here and the impression they gained contributed greatly to us winning the order. For this I would like to thank you all.

However, the fact that nobody in our company spoke Japanese was a problem. As over the next years there will be increased contact with our Japanese colleagues it would be very useful and make a better impression if we did something about this.

We therefore plan to start language courses for all employees who are interested as soon as possible. These courses will be held either before or after work and we would appreciate your thoughts as to when would be best. They will be free of charge.

If you are interested, please contact Janet in the Personnel Department.

QUESTION 10 (ARTICLE)

Work never stops

Ask anyone who lives in Austria," What do you think of when you hear the name Generali Stores?" The answer will be immediate and possibly include words like: 'huge', 'massive choice', 'quality goods', 'knowledgeable staff', 'helpful'. In common with most department stores throughout the world, Generali's existence depends on such a mental picture being in the minds of its customers.

I have worked in department stores for most of my working life and I can recommend a similar career to anyone who has the qualities of hard work, pleasantness and active memory. Those are the minimum qualities needed. If I had to choose the most important of them all, it would have to be 'pleasantness'.

Anyone unable to remain calm and friendly when, for example, a customer cannot decide what to buy should forget any idea of working in a department store. The customer may not 'always be right', but you have to guide him or her gently and tactfully into making a good choice. When customers get home and do not like the goods they have bought, they rarely think it is their fault. In their eyes, YOU are to blame!

Why is an active memory needed? Working in a department store, you must have complete knowledge of all the stock you sell, the whole range available to your customers, and the circumstances in which each variety should be your recommendation. Customers expect you to be able to say immediately what are the strengths and weaknesses of each choice and to advise on which product suits them.

That leaves 'hard work', and believe me, at the end of the working day you will feel tired – very tired! The benefit will be that you will know that your hard work has enabled people to spend their money wisely. How many jobs allow you to be able to say that?

QUESTION 11 (LIST)

List of main points from the article "How a small business can deal with late payment"

A major problem for small firms is late payment by larger firms.

This leads to:
- seeking payments being a daily task
- possibly facing bankruptcy.

Some tactics that can be used include:
- stating terms of payment clearly in contracts
- including in the contracts details of due dates for payments
- offering discounts for early payment
- charging interest on unpaid amounts.

When debts occur:
- always ask for payment
- be polite in such requests
- try to identify a person to contact in the firm that owes money
- if necessary, go to law.

QUESTION 12 (REPORT)

Staff Party

Terms of Reference
Mr Ken Adams, Managing Director, has asked for a report about the recent staff party which was held to thank staff for their help during the company move.

Proceedings
Over a period of 3 days I consulted more than 50 staff and listened to their opinions on the party.

Findings

1 The catering company was chosen on price alone, and was the only one which came within the budget.

2 There was not a lot of food and what there was did not look very fresh.

3 There were too few waiting staff who did not appear to have had any training. They were not very helpful and were not very smartly dressed.

4 The only refreshment available was coffee which was not very hot.

5 All the cutlery was made from plastic and the plates and cups were made from cardboard.

6 No serviettes were provided and the tablecloths were stained.

Conclusions
The catering company provided a very low quality service. They were cheap and the reasons for this were that they had cut costs on food preparation and selection, had used disposable cups and saucers, and had neglected staff training.

Recommendations
I recommend that this company is not used again. For future parties a quality firm should be contracted. This will require an increase in the budget but will be welcomed by all employees.

Your name
Date

QUESTION 13 (LETTER)

Caver House Stationers
48 Halten Road, Plymouth, PL6 2XC
Tel: 01752 506 399 Fax: 01752 500 453

Miss Janet Lawson
Burgess & Cope Solicitors
Callington Way
Tavistock
TK14 3NJ

29 July …

Dear Miss Lawson

Thank you for your order of 25 July.

I have today sent you the following items:

1 pack STICKIT glue sticks	£23.50
2 packs of HB pencils	£6.25 per pack
1 pack large lipped paper clips	£1.75

The LITE box files which you ordered are priced at £55.00 a pack. The price of £50.50 which you quote is last year's price. Please confirm that you wish to order these at the new price.

I have also sent you 9 sets of A-Z board dividers at £1.10 each. Unfortunately this was all we had in stock. We are awaiting delivery of some more and I will send on the remaining set as soon as possible.

The 2 boxes of C4 envelopes at £8.50 each have been sent to you, however, the invoice will detail the correct total of £17.00 for these items.

We do not have any low-noise packaging tape and our suppliers are unable to supply us with any. Please confirm whether we should send normal clear packaging tape or whether you wish to cancel this item.

The 2 packs of YELO post-it notes are priced at £5.75 a pack. The price of £5.50, which you quote, is from last year's catalogue. Please confirm that you wish to order these at the new price.

I have sent you a current catalogue and price list and look forward to hearing from you concerning the above items.

Yours sincerely

your signature

your name
Sales Assistant

QUESTION 14 (LEAFLET)

WELCOME ON BOARD THE WORLD'S LARGEST FAST FERRY

Scotia's fast ferry offers a unique combination of speed, space and comfort all on one deck.

✸ LARGER ✸
120 metres long, 40 metres wide
The size of a football pitch!
Capacity for 1200 passengers & 350 vehicles

✸ FASTER ✸
Travelling at speeds up to 40 knots twice the speed of a conventional ferry
Fast check-in
Up to 5 departures daily

STRANRAER TO BELFAST IN 99 MINUTES

✸ MORE TO DO ✸
Not only is the crossing faster but with so much to do on board time will just flash by:
Entertainment • Live bands • Theme cruises
Bar • Restaurant
Children's entertainers • Kid's play area

Three lounges offering comfortable seating for every passenger.
And remember all facilities are conveniently located on one deck.

Scotia Ferries, Unit 7, Limestone Road Technology Park, Belfast, Co. Antrim, BT15 3AN
Tel: 01232 632 144
Issued on (today's date)

QUESTION 15 (NOTICE)

<u>IMPORTANT NOTICE TO ALL PERSONNEL</u>

1. **PERSONAL INFORMATION**
   It is essential to keep the company informed of any changes to the personal information kept on file. This includes;
   - personal details, eg name, address, telephone number etc
   - bank account details

2. **SIGNING IN AND OUT**
   Many employees are forgetting to sign in and out.
   This is very important and can affect the amount you are paid!
   <u>Please always SIGN IN and SIGN OUT!</u>

3. **STAFF DISCOUNTS**
   We would like to remind all staff that they are entitled to discount on all products;
   - 20% discount for staff who have been employed by us for more than 12 months
   - 15% discount for staff who have been employed by us for less than 12 months

   NB All goods <u>MUST</u> be paid for before taking them home.

4. **LOST PROPERTY**
   If you find anything that does not belong to you please hand it in to the Security Officer.
   If no-one claims it within 6 months, you may claim it for yourself.

A Candidate
(date)

QUESTION 16 (REPORT)

WRF International Fitness Exhibition

22 – 26 February, Berlin

Terms of Reference
Mr Graham Roslin, Sales Manager, has asked me to write a report on the recent WRF exhibition, which took place in Berlin, and to justify the costs involved.

Proceedings
I travelled to Berlin with 3 other sales staff and was present on the stand most of the time. I spoke to the other sales staff to find out about orders they had taken and contacts they had made as a direct result of being at the exhibition.

Findings
1 The exhibition is well-established and is now in its 10th year. This year there were over 175 exhibitors from almost 30 countries. Almost 100,000 visitors were expected to attend.

2 The first 2 days were trade only and many useful contacts were made including two potential distributors for the German market.

3 Multigym equipment was the most popular with trade visitors, particularly the X5 model, which most people thought was very good value and we took over 70 orders for this model.

4 The X4 home gym in particular was well received by the public. They liked the idea that it folded away but wanted to buy from a local distributor.

5 Other contacts from eastern Europe were made, many of whom were interested in distribution, but who wanted very favourable credit terms.

Conclusions
The total value of the orders taken on the stand was just below the total cost involved. Many of these sales were to first-time customers, particularly the trade visitors, and if they are satisfied they will probably place further orders. A lot of useful contacts were made which could result in sales at a later date. Our presence at this exhibition is also very important to establish our company and products on the international market.

Recommendations
I recommend that we continue to take part in this exhibition in future.

Your name
Date

QUESTION 17 (LEAFLET)

DREAM HOLIDAY HOMES IN SPAIN, PORTUGAL AND FRANCE

Self-catering properties

Choose from cosy COTTAGES and splendid VILLAS to renovated FARMHOUSES

All situated in beautiful coastal and countryside locations.

SPECIAL OFFERS FOR NEXT YEAR

Take two separate holidays of a week or more during the next year and get a
20% DISCOUNT
off the price of a second holiday booked.

4 WEEKS FOR THE PRICE OF 3
(available during Low Season)

And don't forget, we can also handle all your travel insurance requirements at highly COMPETITIVE RATES and available from just £50 per annum.

For more information just call FREEPHONE 0990 567 888.

Sims Travel Co., Abbey House, 87 St. John's Street, Luton, Bedfordshire, LU3 1BB
Issued on (today's date)

QUESTION 18 (MEMO)

MEMO

To: All Heads of Faculties
From: Sara Richardson, Deputy Principal
Subject: Presentation Party for Principal
Date: Today's date

As you know Mrs Kirsty Doyle, our College Principal, is retiring at the end of next month after 27 years with the college. A Presentation Party has been arranged for 19th August at 14.30 in the Sinclair Room in the Engineering Faculty. All Heads of Faculties are expected to attend but if you are unable to attend please let me know. Formal dress is requested. A special card, which it is hoped all staff will sign, will be kept in my office until the presentation and can be signed any time during normal working hours.

QUESTION 19 (LIST)

GILBERT'S PORT

1	**The company**	• founded 1815 • expanded since then • now one of the largest port companies worldwide	
2	**Location**	• Vila Nova de Gaia (at mouth of River Douro opposite Oporto)	
3	**Family crest**	• eagle and 3 feathers • appears on labels of every bottle	
4	**History**	1815	founded by Alistair Gilbert – (Scottish)
		1830	Robert Gilbert (son) opened office in London
		1854	Fitzpatrick family brought in to manage Portuguese end
		1861	McNeill family brought in
		Today	member of Fitzpatrick family on the board in Portugal still maintains the feel of a family business
5	**Suppliers**	• farmers (provide grapes and wine) • relationships over many generations • don't have written contracts • shake hands to seal agreements	
6	**Portuguese influence**	• much Portuguese influence • Portuguese MD since 1975 (Gilbert's Portugal)	

QUESTION 20 (LETTER)

Saracen Print Group
17 Hammond Way, Swadlincote, Derby, DY12 6JH
Tel: 01283 550 223 Fax: 01283 550 294 Website: www.saracenprint.co.uk

DERDA
Mr C J Brendan
25 Burton Road
Derby
DY6 6TG

9 September ...

Dear Mr Brendan

Thank you for your letter of 5 September, which we received with great interest.

Saracen Print Group started as a family business in 1966 and now employs over 100 people. Last year the company moved to new purpose-built premises. This includes a large car park directly outside the factory, which provides stress-free parking for customers. At the same time we invested in a state-of-the-art five colour printing press.

All normal printing requirements are undertaken by Saracen and are produced to the highest quality.

Saracen Print Group also has an in-house designer who produces artwork in a ready-to-print form. This avoids technical problems and saves costs for the customer. We offer specialist full-colour printing and also have a full-colour digital printer, which is ideal for personalised printwork in all formats.

We offer competitive rates and guarantee all delivery dates for any work we undertake.

Please contact me if you would like to visit our factory and see samples of the work we do.

I look forward to hearing from you.

Yours sincerely

Pam Lichfield (Ms)
Sales Manager

GLOSSARY

abandon
abroad
absence
absenteeism
absorb
abundance
academically
accept
access
accessible
accident
accommodation
according to
accordingly
accountancy
accounting
accounts
accredited
accurate
acoustics
action
actually
additional
adequate
adequately
administration
administrative assistant
admission
admit
admitted
adult
advanced
advantage
advice
advisable
advise
affect
affected
affordable
agency
agenda
agree to
agreement
air
air-conditioned
airline
airport
aisle
all-day
allow
already
alternatively
ambulance
analyse
anniversary
announce
annual
annual leave
annually
antique
apartment
apologise
apologise for inconvenience
appear
appliance
application
apply
appointment
apprentice
approach
appropriate
approximately
aquarium
architectural
area
arise
around
arrangement
arresting
art
art galley
articles
artist
artistic
artwork
asap
asset
assistant
assured
attend
attended
attraction
automatically
availability
available
avoid
awaiting delivery
award
awarded
aware
back out
background in
back-up
baggage
balanced
balloon
balloon flight
bank holiday
bankrupt
based
based on
basement
behalf
benefit
bin
blend
block of flats
board of directors
boarding
boarding card
bomb
bomb hoax
bonnet
bonus
book
book fair
booking
bookshop
boot
box
box file
branch

branch manager
break
break down
breakdown
brewery
briefly
brilliant
broad
broad range
brochure
browse
budget
buffet
building
building company
bulk
bullets
business
business trip
busy
butter
butter dish
buy
buyer
cabin
calculation
calendar
call centre
camera
cancel
cancellation
candidate
canteen
capital
caption
car
car dealer
card
cardboard
career
careless
carelessness
carpet
carry out
cashmere
casino
casual
casualty
catch
catch up
catering
catering company
catering firm
celebrate
centralise
centre
centuries
certificate
chain
chairman
change
character
characterised
charge
check
check-in
check-out
chemical
cheque book
chief
chief executive officer
children
choice
choose
cinema
cinematographer
clearly
clerk
client
climate
close down
closure
clothing
coach party
coast
colleague
collect
collection
column
comment
commission
common
communicate
communicator
company
company magazine
company policy
compared to
compartment
compensation
competitor
compile
compile a report
complaint
complimentary
components
comprehensive
compressor
computer terminal
computer
concentrated
conception
concern
conclude
conclusion
conditions
conducted tour
conference
conference centre
confidential
confirm
confirmation
confuse
confusion
congratulate
congratulations
consecutive
consider
constantly
construction
consult
consultancy

consumer
contact
contact details
contact lenses
container
contamination
contemporary
contents
contract
contractor
contribute
control
control panel
convenience
convenient
conveniently
conversation
convert
cooking
cooling
cooperation
copier
corporate
corporate colours
corporation
correct
corresponding
cosy
cottage
cotton
countryside
courier
course
course of action
course requirement
courtyard
cover
crafts
create
creature
credit
credit card
credit controller
credit facility
credit note
crest
critical
cross
cross contamination
crowded
cruise
culture
curator
curb
curious
current
currently
customer
customer services manager
customer-friendly
cut off
cutlery
cutting
dairy
damage
damaged
danger
date of birth
date of issue
day
daylight
daylight hours
Dear
Dear Mr
Dear Mrs
Dear Sir/Madam
Dear Sirs
debit card
decade
decision
decrease
deduct
degree
delay
delegate
delegation
delighted
delivery
delivery time
demand
demonstrate
demonstration
depart
department
department head
department store
departure
design
designer
detail
detergent
device
diagram
dictionary
dispenser
diet
digital printing
dinner
direct sales
directions
disaster
disciplinary
disciplinary action
discipline
discount
discuss
dish
dispense
display
dissatisfied
distinguished
distribute
distribution
diver
divide
document
domestic
domestic sales
double
download
draft
dramatically

drawings
dream
dress
driver
driving licence
drum
duration
duties
dye
eagle
earn
ease
economic
education
educational
effect
effective
efficiency
effort
egg tray
electrical goods
electricity
electricity supply
electronics
eligible
emboldening
emergency
employ
employee
employment
enchanting
encircle
enclosed
encounter
encourage
endless
endure
engaged
engineer
engineering
engineering faculty
enjoy
enjoy
enquiry
en-suite
ensure
entertainment
entertainment park
entire
entrance
entry
environment
epidemic
equipment
error
escape
essential
establish
estate office
evaluate
event
examining body
excellent
except
excessive
exchange
exchange goods
exchange rate
exclude
excluding
exclusive
execute
exercise
exhibition
exhibitor
expand
expenses
experience
expert
expertise
explanation
export
export order
extend
extinguisher
extra
extract
eye
eye-catching
eyesight
fabric
facility
factory
factory shop
factual
faculty
faculty head
failure
fair
faithfully
familiar with
familiarise
family
family business
farmer
farmhouse
fascinating
fashion
fast
fast food
faulty
favourable
feather
fee
ferry
fewer
figures
file
filing
finance department
finance director
find
findings
fine
fire
fire brigade
fire extinguisher
firm
first-class
fit
fitness
five-fold

fix
flammable
flat
flavour
fleet
flexibility
flexible
flexitime
flight
flight details
flu epidemic
fluent
foam
foods
football pitch
for sale
force
foregone
foreign
fork-lift truck
formal
formal dress
former
forthcoming
fortnight
forward
founded
fragile
frame
framing
free
free of charge
freephone
freezer
freezing
frequent
fridge freezer
friendly
front cover
frozen
frozen food
fulfil
full-board
full-colour printing
full-time
fund
further
further education
future
gain
gallery
gap
garage
garden
gardener
garment
gate
gather
gauge
generally
generation
get on with
gift
gift voucher
glance
global
glue
gold
goods
government
graduate
graduate programme
grammar
grant
grape
grateful
gratitude
greenhouse
group
growth
guarantee
guest
guidelines
gym
hair product
hall
hallway
hand in
hand luggage
hand out
hand-made
handshake
hands-on
hand-written
hang up
haulage
haulage contractor
head office
heading
health
healthier
healthy
healthy choice
heart disease
helicopter
helpful
helpline
hesitation
history
hoax
hold
holder
holiday
holiday leave
home
hopefully
horizontal
horse
hospital
host
housewife
hurry
identify
ignition
ignition
illness
immediate
imperative
implement
important
impress
impressed

impression
in case of
in operation
in particular
in stock
in the meantime
inclusive
inconvenience
incorporate
increasingly
incredible
independent
individually
inexcusable
inexpensive
influence
informal
information officer
informative
in-house
initials
injured
inner-city
innovations
insert
inspector
install
instruct
instruction
insurance
insurance policy
intended
international
international transfer
internet
internet access
interview
intricacies
invent
invest
invitation
invoice
irrespective
isolated
issue
issued
item
Japanese
jewellery
job
job losses
join
journal
joy
junior
justify
keen
keep an eye on
key
key feature
knitwear
knot
know-how
knowledge
knowledgeable
label
labour
labour charges
lack of
landing
language
language course
language fair
language provider
laptop
latest
lawn
lawsuit
layout
laziness
leaflets
leak
leaking
leather
leave
legal rights
length
lenses
letters
liability
licence
lid
life-long
light refreshment
lightweight
like
limited
liquid
listen to
lists
literature
local
local press
location
lock
logical
long-term
loom
loss
lounge
low
low season
low-noise
loyal
loyalty
loyalty card
luggage
lunch
lunchbreak
luxury
machine
madam
magazine
magnificent
mailing
mailorder catalogue
major
majority
make
make up
manage
management

manager
managing director
manual
manufacture
manufacturer
market research
marketing
marketing manager
marvel
masterpiece
mat
material
mature
meal voucher
meantime
measure
mechanic
mechanical
mechanical failure
medical
medical care
medical goods
medical practice
meet
meeting
memorable
memos
mention
merely
merger
message
mileage
mill
mill shop
mine
miner
mining
mistake
misuse
mobile
model
model agency
modern
mother
motor
multi-media
multi-screen
museum
narrative
nation
national standard
nationwide
naturally
necessary
necessity
neglect
neutral
new
newest
newsletter
nomadic
nomadic tribe
non-dairy
nonslip
normal
normally
notably
note
noticeboard
notices
number
numerous
obese
obligation
observe
obstruct
obvious
occupant
occupy
offer
office
office manager
office supplies
officer
official
OHP
oil
oil painting
oil paints
older
on behalf of
on hold
on-board
on-line
on-screen
operate
operation
operator
opinion
opportunity
optician
option
order
oriental
orientated
originality
outgoing
outlet
out-of-town
outstanding
overhead
overtime
overweight
owe
pack
pack up
packing
packing material
paintbrush
paints
panel
panic
paragraph
park
participant
participate
particular
particularly
partner
part-time
passage
passageway

passengers
passport
pay out
payable
peace
peaceful
pedestrian
people skills
perceived
performance
period
Persian
person
personal assistant
personal liability
personalised
personality
personnel
personnel file
personnel manager
persuade
persuasive
pet
pharmaceuticals
phone
photo session
photocopying
photograph
pick up
picture
pile
pitch
planning
plant
plastic
platform
play
play area
plc
pleasant
points
policy
polite
pollution
popular
population
port
position
postcode
potential
pound
pour
poverty
powder
power
power station
PR agency
practical
practice
praise
precautionary measure
precious
premier
premises
premium
prepaid
prerequisite
presence
presentation
press
press officer
pressure
pressure gauge
prevent
prevention
price
price list
primitive
principal
print
print out
printer
printing
printwork
priority
private
private use
problem
procedure
proceedings
processing
production
professional
profit
programme
project
promote
properly
property
protection
provider
public
public building
public holiday
public transport
publicise
publisher
publishing house
punctual
punctuation
purchase
purpose
purpose-built
qualification
qualified
quarter
question
questionnaire
queue
quotation
quote
rainwater
range
rapidly
rate
rationalisation
ready-made
rearrange
recall
receipt
receiver
receivership

reception
reception area
recipient
recommend
recommendations
record
recruit
recruitment
recruitment agency
redecorate
reduce
redundancy
referee
reference
refill
reflect
refreshment
refund
refurbish
refuse
regional
regional manger
register
regret
regrettable
regular
relate
relationship
relatively
relaxation
relevant
reliable
remainder
remember
remind
remove
renovated
rent
re-open
repair
repeat
repeat order
replace
replacement parts
report
reptile
request
requirement
research
reserved
resolve
resource
respected
response
responsibility
responsible
restaurant
restricted
resulting
retail
retail outlet
retail staff
retailer
retire
retirement
retirement flat
return
return flight
reveal
reverse
reversible
review
reward
ride
rights
risk
roll
roofing
roofing contractor
rubber
rug
rules
rush
safekeeping
safety
safety catch
safety feature
safety inspector
safety officer
safety record
safety training
sailing
salad
sale
sales
sales department
sales figures
sales goods
sales person
sales representative
satisfactory
satisfied
sauna
saving
scale
scale model
schedule
school party
screen
seal
season
season ticket
seating
secretary
section
security check
sedentary
seem
select
selected
selection
self-catering
self-confident
self-service
self-study
semi-conductor
seminar
sender
senior
sense
separate
serial number

serious
serve
service
serviceability
serviette
session
set
settings
shake
shake hands
share
shark
sheepdog
sheet
shoe retailer
shop
shop around
shoplifting
short
short break
short-sleeved
show round
showroom
side entrance
sign
signal
signal failure
signature
significant
simplicity
sincerely
single
single mother
sir
sister company
site
situation
sketch board
skills
slight
slogan
smart
smooth
snack
software
software company
solarium
solicitor
solution
source
space
special
special event
special offer
special rate
specialise
specialising in
specially
species
specification
specimen
spectacles
speech
spelling
spill
splendid
sports
sports club
sports equipment
sports personality
spray
stable
staff
staff turnover
stage
stall
stand
standard
statement
state-of-the-art
stationers
steal
steam bath
steering column
stock
stock record
stockbroker
storage
store
store manger
straight
strength
stress
stress-free
strike
strong pound
structure
student
sturdy
subject
subject to availability
subjects
sub-section
succession
sudden
sufficient
suggest
suggestion
suit
suitability
suitable
superb
superior
supervision
supervisor
supplies
supply
surf
surface
surrounded
survey
suspicious
switch
symbol
tablecloths
tactful
tactfully
take advantage of
take care of
take over
take place
take-off

tape
target
task
taste
tax clerk
tax inspector
taxation
tax-free
technical
technique
technology
telecommunications
telephone banking
telephone operator
telephone voice
temperature
tender
tent
terminal
terminate
terms
terms & conditions
terms of reference
textbook
theme
theme park
thermostat
third party
thread
throughout
ticket
tilting
time
time-saving
tip
tipping
title
token
top
top priority
topical
total
tour
tour operator
tourist
tourist information
tournament
towel
town hall
trade
trade fair
tradition
traditional
trainee
training
training course
training officer
tranquillity
transaction
transfer
transport
travel
travel agent
traveller
tray
treat
treatment
tremendous
trend
trial
tribe
triple
tripled
tumble drying
turbine
Turkish
turn away
turn off
turn on
turnover
unacceptable
unattractive
unbeatable
under licence
underfed
underline
unfortunately
unique
unit
unit price
universal
unnecessary
unusual
upcoming
upright
urgent
use
used
used car
user
user's manual
usual
utmost
valid
valuables
value
variety
vary
vegetable
vegetable dye
vegetarian
vehicle
ventilation
venue
version
vet
video camera
villa
visitor
voice
voluntary
voluntary redundancy
voucher
wages
wages department
walk
walled
wanted
warehouse
warning
washer dryer
washing

washing powder
wastage
wastepaper
water
water supply
water turbine
watercolour
weave
weaver
weaving
weaving loom
web page
website
wedding
welcome
well-dressed
well-equipped
well-established
well-known
wheelchair
whether
whole
wife
wild
willing
woollen
woollen trade
work
work placement
workbook
workforce
working environment
workmen
workshop
worldwide
worn
younger
yours faithfully
yours sincerely

LCCI International Qualifications

Sample Examination Paper 2

ENGLISH FOR BUSINESS

Level 2

Subject Code: 2041

Time allowed: **2 hours 30 minutes**

INSTRUCTIONS FOR CANDIDATES

- Answer **all 3** questions. You should only answer **one** option in **question 1**.
- All answers should be correctly numbered, but do not need to be in numerical order.
- There is credit for correct spelling, punctuation and grammar.
- You need to communicate appropriately and well.
- Check your work carefully.
- You may use an English or bilingual dictionary.

QUESTION 1

Answer ONE of the following options:

OPTION (A)

Situation: You are employed in a large store.

The manager suggests that you should **write an article** describing how important customer service is to a business. He says, "Our staff magazine, *Business Sense*, has been asking staff to contribute articles that describe what they think are the most important things to remember when dealing with customers and clients … The editor of the magazine prefers articles to be 4 or 5 paragraphs long … I think you will be able to write an interesting and informative article … I have noticed how well you deal with our customers. Don't forget to think of a title for the article."

You write down some ideas of what you may want to include in the article:

- happy customer/client = business success — service good – customer MAY tell others; service bad – customer WILL tell others
- customer expects: respect, our being helpful, etc
  being able to trust advice, product, service etc
  pleasant atmosphere – smile
  courtesy
- If you don't look after customers/clients, COMPETITORS WILL.
- Every contact is possible customer – be pleasant, offer help (if possible)
- NOTE – I many want to leave out some of these ideas AND/OR add to them

Task

Write the article. **(40 marks)**

OPTION (B)

Situation:

For the past year the firm for which you work, Darbar Industries, Lahore, Pakistan, has used teleconferences (meetings using telephones instead of participating 'face-to-face') for most of its meetings. Mr Bashir Javed, the Director of Administration, asks you to **write a report** on what the staff, who have taken part in the teleconferences, think of the system. He says, "Obviously, there are advantages and disadvantages. Saving money on travel is one advantage – an important one! We have factories and offices all over the world – with teleconferences we can regularly hold meetings with any or all of our branches. Let me have the report by the end of next month. Make some recommendations on how we can improve the efficiency of the teleconferences."

You have sent a questionnaire by email to all branches of Darbar Industries asking them to distribute it to all staff who have taken part in a teleconference. Here are the notes that you make of the most frequent comments you received in the replies:

….Option B continued on next page

Question 1 Option B continued

Easy to attend – including guest speakers. Less socialising – more time on agenda. Saves money.

Often more preparation time needed – BUT participants better prepared!

Technical failures + organiser's lack of knowledge of equipment = problems!

GOOD for simple problem solving + exchanging information.

LESS GOOD = negotiation + it is VERY IMPERSONAL
+ time difference in other countries.

Several recommendations for occasional face-to-face meetings.
("It is easier to talk to people over the phone, if you already know them.")

Task

Write the report. **(40 marks)**

OPTION (C)

Situation:

You work for THK Steel Products in Brisbane, Australia. Mr Brian Murdoch, the Sales Manager, is about to visit potential clients throughout Europe. He asks you to phone and confirm a provisional booking that you made 3 months earlier with Hotel de Charenton, Paris, France.

Here is a transcript of the telephone conversation:

You	*This is THK Steel Products of Brisbane, Australia. I wish to check a provisional booking for Wednesday and Thursday nights next week.*
Hotel	*Let me see … THK Steel Products … yes … there is a single room reserved for a Mr Murdoch.*
You	*Mr Murdoch is our Sales Manager. Is the room en-suite?*
Hotel	*All our rooms are en-suite.*
You	*Mr Murdoch will need to work from his room and he will find it difficult to do so if there is any noise.*
Hotel	*Mr Murdoch will not be disturbed. His room overlooks our courtyard. It is very quiet and peaceful. By the way, since Mr Murdoch will need to work while he is staying with us, does he know that we offer all modern business facilities to our customers?*
You	*You mean internet access …*
Hotel	*… anything you would expect to be available - even a person to assist him, but we obviously have to charge extra for that. All our other services are free.*
You	*You have been very helpful. I would like to confirm the booking. Mr Murdoch will need dinner both days.*
Hotel	*We don't provide meals – except for breakfast. We do, however, have arrangements with the restaurant next door to us. Let us know if you still wish us to book meals for Mr Murdoch.*

Write a memo to Mr Murdoch and give him the details of the arrangements.

Task

Write the memo. **(40 marks)**

QUESTION 2

Situation: Mrs. Christine Williams, the Manager of Clarity Computer Sales, asks you to reply to the following letter which she has received. She suggests that you should check the details given by Mr Fenton. She says, "Arrange to fix the problem with the computer immediately. Dissatisfied customers are bad publicity for us. However, the Johnson 177 laser printer will only print in black. That should have been made clear to Mr Fenton when it was given to him. The Johnson 277 prints in colour. Tell him that we can supply the 277 at £180 extra."

Tel: 01343 595950

17 Lancaster Road
Exeter
Devon
EX6 8YH

Clarity Computer Sales plc
134 - 138 High Road
Exeter
Devon
EX2 3SG

15 November ....

Dear Sir or Madam

In March of this year, I bought an Aspect 9200 computer from you. Additionally, as a special offer, you gave me a Johnson 177 laser printer free of charge.

Neither the computer nor the printer works adequately. The computer constantly switches itself off and the printer refuses to print in colour!

I phoned you last week and complained about the computer. I was told that I could bring the computer into Clarity Computer Sales and your "expert" would look at it for me. As I told your employee on the phone, I expect someone to come to my home. I do not intend to come to you! You are at fault, not me!

Please do something very soon! Otherwise I shall get in touch with the local newspapers to tell them what poor service I have had from you.

Yours faithfully

Michael Fenton

Michael Fenton

QUESTION 2 CONTINUED

You look at the agreement that Mr Fenton signed. Here is an extract from it:

➲ Clarity Computer Sales plc agrees to visit the customer's home to repair any product, if a fault is reported within 6 months of purchase.

➲ Clarity Computer Sales plc agrees to repair any product brought to its premises within 12 months of purchase.

➲ All such repairs will be conducted free of charge (parts and labour).

In discussion with Mrs. Williams, you decide that the repair, as a goodwill gesture, will be carried out at Mr Fenton's home.

Task

Write the letter. **(30 marks)**

QUESTION 3

Situation

You work for Rockley Enterprises, Bridgetown, Barbados, West Indies. Mr Leon Eastwood, Managing Director, says to you that he is interested in an article he has read in *The Bridgetown Business Observer*, a local magazine. He asks you to **write a list** of the main points of the article. "It will be useful when I next have a discussion session with our trainee managers."

Here is the article:

What do you expect from your staff and what do they expect from you?

If you want the best from your workers, you have to plan for it. Are you sure that your members of staff know what you expect them to do? Don't leave them to guess what you want from them. Tell them in as much detail as possible so that there is very little guessing involved.

Employees also need "room to grow". What do I mean by that? Well, they need challenges, tasks that stretch them, jobs from which they gain new knowledge and expertise. Sometimes this will involve formal training, but often it will simply be a matter of learning through doing the task. A staff that always works within its known capabilities is a staff that has no ambition, and a firm that has employees with no ambition is a firm that will itself not improve.

Praise your workers if a job is done well. Recognition from employers is often more important than extra money – although that is welcome too! Equally, you should let staff know if a job is not done as well as you need.

Require people to prepare themselves whether it is for a major new role in the firm or simply for a weekly meeting. When people fail to prepare themselves for meetings, it implies that the work attitude in the firm is quite possibly inadequate. Do something about it. Speak to anyone who is obviously ill-prepared and make it very clear that your expectations are higher.

Task

Write the list. **(30 marks)**

ANSWERS
SAMPLE EXAMINATION PAPER 1

QUESTION 1
Option A

MEMO

To	Mrs. Harris, Managing Director
From	A. Candidate
Subject	Preliminary Information for Visits to our Casablanca Office
Date	*Today's Date*

Colleagues going to our new Moroccan base need to be aware that French is spoken most often and few residents are fluent in English. We have the services of our own representative in Casablanca, Yves Roland, who will help with any communication difficulties.

Visas are not necessary for UK citizens, but all passports must be valid for at least 6 months beyond the date of arriving in Morocco.

There are flights directly to and from Birmingham Airport taking between 5 and 7 hours. (The regulations for entry into Morocco require all visitors to have a return ticket.) A journey from the airport at Casablanca to the city centre by taxi will take about 40 minutes.

Casablanca has many good hotels, but we have received recommendations for Hotel Le Royal Mansour.

I can supply more detailed information, including how to contact Yves Roland or make bookings at the Hotel Le Royal Mansour, to anyone needing it.

A.C.

QUESTION 1

Option B

USERS' VIEWS ON THE CHILDREN'S LIBRARY AT GREENFIELD PUBLIC LIBRARY:

Terms of Reference

A request was made for a report on users' opinions of the facilities offered by the Children's Library. The report is to be available for the next meeting of the Library Committee.

Procedure

For 4 weeks all older children using the Children's Library and adults accompanying younger children were asked to write down their comments and to make recommendations for improvement.

Findings

300 users in total provided views: 212 older children and 88 adults.

OLDER CHILDREN	-	criticized the shortage of study space for homework
	-	complained of the high noise levels in the Children's Library.
ADULTS	-	praised the Saturday storytelling sessions
	-	expressed general satisfaction with facilities for younger children.
MANY USERS	-	were concerned at the lack of study facilities • desks, tables at which to write • access to computers and photocopiers.
	-	were dissatisfied with the late opening and early closing of the Children's Library.

Conclusions

- The opening and closing times are causing problems to some users.
- The study/homework arrangements are seen as inadequate.
- Access to computers and photocopiers is insufficient.
- The storytelling time is popular.
- The younger users are reasonably well catered for.
- The noise levels are problematic for the older children.

Recommendations

GENERAL	Retain storytelling sessions. Investigate the viability of changing opening and closing times.
SHORT TERM	Provide additional computers. Increase the number of tables. Improve availability of photocopying.
LONG TERM	Investigate possibility of a study room separate from but adjacent to the Children's Library.

A. Candidate
Date

QUESTION 1

Option C

Every hour of every working day is different

Wednesday, 11 June 2007 is a date I shall never forget. That was the day that I began my job at Bartlett Department Store in Birmingham. I was warned at interview that at the end of my first day I would feel more tired than I had ever felt before. But no warning could ever have prepared me for the actual experience. Don't misunderstand me – I love my job and I look forward each day to coming to work. However, by 6 o'clock that first evening all I wanted to do was to drag myself home, go to bed and sleep for a week.

The day had started at 8 a.m. with a short introduction to the department in which I would start: Men's Clothing. I was told that I would be working with the Senior Sales Assistant, Clive Ault. When I was introduced to Clive, he said, "Don't worry. I'll show you what to do and gradually let you do things yourself. You will soon learn." At that exact moment, the entrance doors opened and in walked the first customer of the thousands that I was to meet in my career. I remember him well. He ignored Clive, came straight towards me, stating very forcibly and angrily that I had sold him a pair of trousers some days ago and when he had gone home, his wife had disliked the colour. My mouth moved but no sound came out!

Watching Clive deal with the situation made me full of admiration for his skills of diplomacy and tact. Without ever saying that the customer was mistaken, he apologised, explained that I had started only that day, and that I looked very similar to a previous assistant who no longer worked at Bartlett. He then replaced the trousers with a pair of a colour that was "certain to be more acceptable", exchanged pleasantries with the customer, offered any future help necessary and closed with, "Should your good lady prefer a different colour, there will be no problem." The customer left completely satisfied and even apologised to me for his mistaking my identity. I had learned my first lesson in selling: "Never tell customers directly that they are wrong – even when they are."

That day and the succeeding days I learned many further practical lessons: the importance of knowing your stock, how to help customers choose goods that are suitable for them, how to combat tiredness, how to work for 8 to 10 hours and only sit down when having a coffee break or lunch, and the rewards of doing a worthwhile job in which each day you meet many different people.

Because you are reading this, I know that you are thinking of applying for a job at Bartlett. I genuinely encourage you to do so. Bartlett offers training, job satisfaction, decent pay, and the possibility to be considered for promotion. There is in my opinion no better place to work, but I give you the same warning that I received: "You will feel more tired at the end of your first day than you have ever felt before." Remember too that there are many "Clives" at Bartlett to advise you, to encourage you and to step in when needed.

QUESTION 2

Joynton Electrical and Electronic Supplies
43 Kent Street Sydney NSW 2000

Mrs. Marcelle Kemmis
19 Lawson Square
Redfern
NSW 2012

Today's Date

Dear Mrs. Kemmis

Radio left at our Erskineville Branch for repair:

We are sorry that you have had so much difficulty in finding out what has happened to your radio and apologise for any lapses in our usually efficient communications.

When the Erskineville Branch was severely damaged by fire, we tried to contact customers who had property at the shop. Unfortunately, our records were destroyed together with much of our stock. We had no way of knowing who had left items there to be repaired and therefore could not contact you as soon as we would have liked.

Woolloomalloo Branch took over all the goods and responsibilities that we could salvage or trace from Erskineville. Unhappily, it appears that your radio was not among the items that were able to be saved.

If you can supply me with details of the make and model of your radio, I shall be happy to supply you with a replacement and deliver it to you free of charge.

Again I apologise for the inconvenience that you have suffered. Let me have the necessary information so that I can rectify the situation quickly and, please, contact me directly if our apologies and suggestions are not acceptable to you.

Yours sincerely

A. Candidate

A……. Candidate
Customer Liaison Officer

QUESTION 3

<u>Older customers are valuable customers</u>

1. The fastest growing market sector is the older generation.

2. Companies need a strategy to target this consumer group. This should include:

- training sales staff to be aware of "senior" customers' preferences
- creating advertisements specifically for this group
  - using models of the same age group
  - placing adverts in magazines read by this age group
- providing somewhere quiet for a sale to be discussed
- giving written information
- not using sales "tricks"

3. Don't underestimate the importance of after-sales service. This should include:

- issuing honest guarantees and warranties
- contacting customers directly for feedback on goods and/or services
- rectifying problems and faults promptly and willingly.

ANSWERS
SAMPLE EXAMINATION PAPER 2

QUESTION 1

Option A

GOOD CUSTOMER SERVICE IS GOOD BUSINESS

Customer service is easily the most important thing to concentrate on in a business. The treatment of customers by a firm can be good; too often it is dreadful. When you come across what you think is unacceptable treatment from a business, you simply do not want to give that business any more custom. It is often surprising to me to see how bad customer service can be in some firms and how their management does not seem to be worried about it. Fortunately, our own management knows that we must aim to have customers who are delighted with our service.

For people to be 'delighted' with customer service, and not simply satisfied, means the customer service has to be so good that customers tell others about how wonderful our business is. There is a saying that an unhappy customer will tell 20 people about the experience. However, we want people, who experience our customer service, and are so delighted that they will want to tell 20 people of their great pleasure with our service.

How do we focus on customer service to produce delighted customers? The answer is in concentrating on their needs and wants. Many of these needs and wants are obvious. To be happy, customers expect: 1. to be treated with respect and importance 2. to be greeted with a smile 3. to find understanding of their problems 4. to meet standards of service that can be relied on 5. to be treated fairly in terms of price and service.

To achieve all these expectations, we need to make sure that at every staff meeting the first thing on the agenda is a discussion on how to improve customer service. It is important to communicate to all employees that if we do not serve our customers, a competitor will.

We should do a customer survey at least once a year. This will provide useful feedback and remind customers that we are committed to their satisfaction. We must not assume that the absence of complaints means that we are doing a good job. Many customers do not complain; they just go to our competition. By surveying the customers on a regular basis we can detect a problem before it becomes impossible to deal with. Through emphasising customer service we will meet and exceed our customers' expectations. That is good business sense by anyone's definition!

QUESTION 1

Option B

Staff views on the use of teleconferences at Darbar Industries:

Terms of Reference

The report was requested by Mr Bashir Javed and is to be available by the end of December..

Procedure

A questionnaire was designed and distributed via email to all branches with the instruction that it should be completed by all staff who had taken part in a teleconference. All completed questionnaires were to be returned to A. Candidate.

Findings

Strengths of teleconferences	Attendance is easy. Little time is spent in socialising. Running costs are low. Attendees seem well prepared for meetings. Teleconferences are seen as most suitable for the exchange of information and solving simple problems.
Weaknesses of teleconferences	Large amount of time is spent by attendees in preparation. Technical problems hinder smooth running. Teleconferences are described as 'impersonal'. They are considered less suited to situations involving negotiation.

Conclusions

- Benefits are considerable.
- The effects of the weaknesses can be lessened.

Recommendations

1. Teleconferencing should continue as the main form of meeting.
2. Improved training in solving technical problems is required.
3. Occasional face-to-face meetings are advisable especially when complex negotiations are likely.

A.Candidate

Appropriate date.

QUESTION 1

Option C

MEMO

To Mr Murdoch
From A. Candidate
Date 17 November ….

Room booking at Hotel de Charenton, Paris

As you asked, I have confirmed that there is a room booked for you at Hotel de Charenton for Wednesday and Thursday of next week.

The room is en-suite and overlooks a pleasant courtyard. I was assured that the room is suitably quiet for your work to be undisturbed.

The hotel staff was keen to point out that Hotel de Charenton offers its guests the use of fully modern business facilities free of charge. If you require an assistant, that too can be arranged but a fee is payable for this service.

Breakfast is served at the hotel but other meals are not available. The restaurant next door to de Charenton will provide meals by prior booking.

Please let me know if you want me to order dinner there for you, or if there are any further arrangements you wish me to make.

A.C.

QUESTION 2

Clarity Computer Sales plc
134 – 138 High Road, Exeter, Devon, EX2 3SG

Mr Michael Fenton
17 Lancaster Road
Exeter
Devon
EX6 8YH

17 November ....

Dear Mr Fenton

We are sorry that you feel you have had cause to complain about our service and products. The information given to you about the repair to your computer was accurate. Our agreement allows for home repair only if the fault is reported to us within 6 months of purchase. However, as a special gesture to you we shall nevertheless arrange for the repair to be carried out at your home. No charge will be made.

The Johnson 177 printer that was issued does only print in black. The Johnson 277 prints in colour and black. It costs an additional £180.

We hope that these arrangements will make amends for our lack of communication. Please let me know if we can be of any further help to you and if you wish us to replace the Johnson 177 with the 277 version.

Yours sincerely

Y. Name

Your Name
Assistant Manager

QUESTION 3

<u>Stimulating ambition among staff</u>

For greatest efficiency members of staff need to:
- know what is expected of them
- be informed in detail what each task involves.

To stimulate the interest of staff:
- ask them to do jobs that make demands on them
    - new skills
    - new knowledge
- train them
    - formally through courses
    - informally as part of a task.

They should be:
- praised when the job is done well
- informed when the performance is below expectation.

Staff need to be encouraged to prepare for:
- routine tasks
- new roles